Grace, The Gift, and Living a Life of Faith

Workbook 1

of the series,
Living a Supernatural Life Naturally

by Linda Morgan

Grace, The Gift, and Living a Life of Faith

Workbook 1

of the series,

Living a Supernatural Life Naturally

by Linda Morgan

Grace, The Gift, and Living a Life of Faith by Linda Morgan
Part One of the series, *Living a Supernatural Life Naturally*

ISBN 978-1-954509-12-2

Scriptures marked CEV are taken from the CONTEMPORARY ENGLISH VERSION (CEV): Scripture taken from the CONTEMPORARY ENGLISH VERSION copyright© 1995 by the American Bible Society. Used by permission.

Scriptures marked HCSB are taken from the HOLMAN CHRISTIAN STANDARD BIBLE (HCSB): Scripture taken from the HOLMAN CHRISTIAN STANDARD BIBLE, copyright© 1999, 2000, 2002, 2003 by Holman Bible Publishers, Nashville Tennessee. All rights reserved.

Scriptures marked NIV are taken from the NEW INTERNATIONAL VERSION (NIV): Scripture taken from THE HOLY BIBLE, NEW INTERNATIONAL VERSION ®. Copyright© 1973, 1978, 1984, 2011 by Biblica, Inc.™. Used by permission of Zondervan.

Scriptures marked ESV are taken from the THE HOLY BIBLE, ENGLISH STANDARD VERSION (ESV): Scriptures taken from THE HOLY BIBLE, ENGLISH STANDARD VERSION ® Copyright© 2001 by Crossway, a publishing ministry of Good News Publishers. Used by permission.

Scriptures marked NKJV are taken from the NEW KING JAMES VERSION (NKJV): Scripture taken from the NEW KING JAMES VERSION®. Copyright© 1982 by Thomas Nelson, Inc. Used by permission. All rights reserved.

Quotations designated (NET) are from the NET Bible® copyright ©1996-2016 by Biblical Studies Press, L.L.C. http://netbible.com All rights reserved. Scripture quoted by permission. The names: THE NET BIBLE®, NEW ENGLISH TRANSLATION COPYRIGHT (c) 1996 BY BIBLICAL STUDIES PRESS, L.L.C. NET Bible® IS A REGISTERED TRADEMARK THE NET BIBLE® LOGO, SERVICE MARK COPYRIGHT (c) 1997 BY BIBLICAL STUDIES PRESS, L.L.C. ALL RIGHTS RESERVED

Cover photo credit: istockphoto.com/loeskieboom

Printed in the United States
visionrun.com

About the Author

Linda Morgan

Linda Morgan is a wife, mother, grandmother, business owner, and gifted Christian teacher. She is well known for her ability to express spiritual principles in everyday language. After being introduced to the person of the Holy Spirit in the 1970s, she has spent the years since then studying and sharing what she's learned with others.

She has ministered and taught in churches in the U.S. at retreats, through keynote addresses, and on mission trips to Europe and Central America. Linda has also had a personal prayer ministry for hurting people for over thirty years. She is passionate about helping others resolve inner and outer conflict through prayers that heal the heart and change lives.

As a business owner, she also consults and speaks to individuals and professionals alike on the importance of first impressions and works with clients on wardrobe, color, style, and makeup.

Linda and her husband Dell make their home in Knoxville, Tennessee. They have been married since 1972 and have two grown children and seven grandchildren.

Introduction to the Series, Living a Supernatural Life Naturally

For about thirty years prior to developing the material for this study, I had been involved in leading women's ministries. I sensed the Lord was telling me in 2011 that it was time to rest and recharge my spiritual batteries. It seemed He was telling me it was time to take care of myself physically and build up my spiritual man. I needed a time that involved *being* instead of *doing*.

So, after pulling back from leading in our church for a season, I sensed the Lord saying it was time to get involved again. I began praying and asking Him what my purpose was now. It seemed He immediately spoke to my heart saying "I want you to teach a Bible Study in the fall. The title is *Living a Supernatural Life Naturally*, and here are the ten topics." You can imagine that I immediately felt overwhelmed, but He reminded me I had already taught most of those subjects over the years. So, I've incorporated the ten topics into six workbooks: the first two have three topics each, followed by four single-topic workbooks.

The purpose of this study is to bring an increased awareness, appreciation for, and understanding of the ministry of the Holy Spirit in our daily lives. The goal is to bring us deeper into His presence through the ministry of the Holy Spirit. We want to develop a listening ear that enables us to respond more readily to the still, quiet voice of the Spirit in our everyday lives.

We can know the Holy Spirit as a Person of the Godhead and not just think of Him as an impersonal influence in our lives. We want to begin to live supernaturally through the power of the Holy Spirit working in us to accomplish God's purposes by fully living the Christ life.

–Linda Morgan

Contents

Living a Supernatural Life Naturally: Course Overview

Workbook 1: Grace, The Gift, and Living a Life of Faith

Grace is not just God's favor; it is also His empowerment to us so that we can overcome our weakness and sin to do His will (Romans 6:14). Everyone who has grace has the Holy Spirit living in them and can live a supernatural life naturally. Jesus wants to live His life through us, as us.

The Gift of the Holy Spirit was sent to us as a Helper. The Holy Spirit is a Person, not just an impersonal influence. Jesus did not leave us helpless (John 14:26, 15:26). Being filled with the Spirit is continual (Ephesians 5:18). Spiritual gifts are supernatural manifestations of God's power provided by the Holy Spirit.

Living a Life of Faith is like a mustard seed that must be planted, watered, fertilized, protected, and pruned. True spiritual life flows from our spirit and affects our mind. Faith is a gift of grace. Faith is taking that first step without seeing what is ahead. Faith occurs when we stop trying to do something by our own efforts and trust the Lord to do it for us. Belief and faith are not the same. Acting on our belief means we have faith.

Workbook 2: Prayer and Obedience

The Power of Prayer happens when we believe that God is and that He rewards those who seek Him. Answered prayer affirms us (Hebrews 11:6). We pray because we believe (have faith) and hope that prayer changes things. Prayer is not overcoming God's reluctance but embracing His willingness.

Listening Prayer is when the Holy Spirit leads and guides us into all truth. We have to develop a listening ear (John 16:13). God speaks to us both indirectly and directly; He is always speaking, but we are not always listening. God speaks to us and through us (1 Corinthians 12).

Obedience Isaiah 1:19 says if we are willing and obedient, we will eat the good of the land. Obedience brings revelation (John 14:6). It is a key to destiny, which comes faster when we are obedient. Grace empowers us to live a life of obedience, and it empowers us to live beyond our abilities (John 21:15-17).

Living in the age of the New Testament means we are covered by grace and are under a new covenant. A covenant that means we don't have to work and struggle because we can rest in what Christ has provided. *We have the gift of the Holy Spirit, the very presence of Jesus living in us and enabling us to live a supernatural life, naturally.* It requires trusting that He is doing just that, and we don't have to make things happen. We pray, listen, and obey what the Spirit is saying. If we make a mistake and miss it (and sometimes we will), we confess, repent, and ask Him to empower us to do better. He has delegated spiritual authority to us, and when our hearts are right and our motives are pure, we can be effective over the enemy.

Workbook 3: Spiritual Authority

To defeat the enemy, we must realize and believe we have been given authority in the spirit realm. The blood of Jesus and His resurrection defeats the enemy once and for all. We operate from a place of victory because He has already won and delegated His authority to believers. We have been given authority in the spirit realm, which enables us to win our battles in the natural realm too. This is how we live supernaturally, naturally.

Workbook 4: Spiritual Warfare

Spiritual warfare can sound violent or challenging, but it's actually neither. It's simply recognizing the enemy and defeating him through prayer, while using the Sword of the Spirit — the Word of God — against him. We do need to understand Satan's strategy in order to know how to defeat him. To do that, we must realize and believe we have been given authority in the spirit realm. We are more than conquerors (Romans 8:37; 1 John 4:4)!

Workbook 5: Healing Prayer

We often think of healing prayer as one of the 1 Corinthians 12 gifts for healing the body given by the Holy Spirit. But healing prayer as we're discussing it, is about healing the heart. Any Christian can use this workbook, either individually or in partnership with a few others, to allow the Spirit to touch and begin to heal deeply wounded places in our hearts. It's a powerful tool to help find victory and healing to experience a more vibrant walk. In short, it's a path to emotional and spiritual healing.

Workbook 6: Destiny and Inheritance

It's difficult to arrive at your destiny according to God's plan for your life and leave a legacy, if you don't know who God created you to be. *Destiny and Inheritance* is a workbook about agreeing with God and discovering His path for you. Once you know God's plan for your life, the next challenge involves overcoming the obstacles keeping you from living it out. It requires learning to rest in the assurance that God has a special design for your life, a unique destiny and inheritance beyond anything you could have imagined.

Topic One: Grace

Grace is not just God's favor; it is also His empowerment so that we can overcome our weakness and sin to do His will.

Romans 6:14: *for sin will have no dominion over you, since you are not under the law but under grace.*

Lesson 1: New Covenant Grace

It's often said that mercy is *not getting* what we deserve, while grace *is getting* what we don't deserve.

If you've ever watched the movie, attended the play, or read Victor Hugo's classic novel, *Les Miserable*, you've seen what grace and mercy can do to change a life.

In the first scenes from the 2012 movie, we see a perfect picture of the grace of God. In the opening scene, Jean Val Jean is serving time in a hard labor camp for stealing bread to feed his sister's children. After he is released, he is hungry and dirty, with no hope of finding food or shelter.

A bishop takes him in for the night, feeds him dinner, and gives him a place to sleep. The housekeeper doesn't approve, doesn't trust him, and is also afraid of him. During the night, he gets up and robs the cupboards of the silver they used on the dinner table. The bishop comes in while he is filling his bag, and Val Jean hits him and knocks him down before escaping.

After he leaves, the police immediately see him with the bag and know he has stolen the contents. When they take him back, the bishop says that not only did he give the silver to him, but that Val Jean had forgotten the candlesticks and proceeded to give him those too. In the film, you can see how surprised he is at the undeserved kindness of the bishop.

He deserved punishment, but the bishop showed mercy. While he deserved punishment, he didn't get it (mercy). He also kept his freedom (grace), getting what he didn't deserve.

This scene in the movie is such a picture of God's grace as unearned, unmerited favor for us. As a result, Jean Val Jean went on to try to repay the kindness by living a life exhibiting the fruit of the Spirit. (I would recommend watching this entire movie. It is such a portrayal of grace, mercy, and forgiveness.)

Because of the bishop's grace, Val Jean was transformed into another man who showed others mercy throughout the rest of his life. This is an example of God changing someone from the inside out through forgiveness and grace. Because he was given mercy and saved, the fruit of the Spirit became evident in his life. He was bought with silver and given back to God as a new man. It is the same for us. The bishop showed faith in Jean Val Jean to live life as a different person, and he empowered him through forgiveness. He was delivered from fear. That is what God has done for us through the gift of salvation.

The Holy Spirit empowers us to live differently.

Grace is referred to as the unmerited favor of God. (NKJ) The Greek word for *grace* is *charis,* defined as "a favor done without payback, an unearned, unmerited favor." Ephesians 2:8 *it is by grace we are saved through faith and not of ourselves.* It is a gift from God. Romans 3:24 we are justified freely because of grace through redemption. Hebrews 12:28 (NKJ) *Since we are receiving a kingdom which cannot be shaken, let us have grace, by which we may serve God acceptably with reverence and awe.* Grace enables us to serve God in a way that is pleasing and acceptable to Him, and it looks different in each of us. The way I serve God may look different from the way you serve God. He has always been full of grace, but with the introduction of the Holy Spirit at Pentecost, grace works in us at a whole new level thanks to the infilling of the Holy Spirit. This is new covenant grace.

Discussion:

What would it look like to serve God without grace?

New Covenant grace is God's faith in man because, through the Holy Spirit, He has given us power to be a witness for Him. Peter is a good example of New Covenant grace. Before the Holy Spirit came, he denied Jesus three times. After receiving the Holy Spirit, he boldly preached to thousands on the Day of Pentecost. At Pentecost, the Holy Spirit descended on the people in the upper room and empowered them to be a witness for Christ.

God will do the same for us. All we have to do is ask for everything He has for us. He doesn't show partiality, so we will receive what we ask for, however, it requires a total surrender of our will (Luke 11:13/Acts 10:34). We have to give up any ideas of what we think our lives should look like or what we are willing to accept. Sometimes our misconceptions are a hindrance.

Discussion:

How could our misconceptions hinder how we receive the fullness of the Holy Spirit operating in and through us?

Prayer*: Father, I repent of my sins and ask you, Jesus, to come into my heart and live your life through me, as me. I confess that you are Lord. I ask you, Jesus, to baptize me in the Holy Spirit, empowering me to be a witness for you. Thank you for doing it. Amen.*

Grace is always marked by God's enabling work within us to overcome our helplessness. When we don't know what to say, the Holy Spirit will speak through us. If we open our mouth,

He will fill it (Psalm 81:10; Ezekiel 29:21). In 1 Corinthians 15:10, it says that grace gives us the ability to do His will. In Galatians 2:20, it says I am crucified with Christ, now He lives His life through me because I have been resurrected with Him as a new creation. Jesus wants to live His life through us, as us. That will look different for each of us, but it will produce the same fruit in all of us that we see in Galatians 5:22, which is love, joy, peace, forbearance, kindness, goodness, faithfulness, gentleness, and self-control.

All the grace we need.

How is it possible that, as Christians, we already have all the grace we need? It is possible because it is a gift from the Holy Spirit. Theologian Watchman Nee[1] declared the following, "Everyone who has grace has the Holy Spirit living in them."

"The secret of a Christian's life is that the supernatural becomes natural in him as a result of the grace of God, and the experience of this becomes evident in the practical, everyday details of life, not in times of intimate fellowship with God." -Oswald Chambers, author, *My Utmost for His Highest*

Grace is not just God's favor; it is also His empowerment so that we can overcome our weakness and sin to do His will. Jesus gives us access by faith to this grace, which gives us the ability to please God. It is supernatural. Romans 6:14

The Holy Spirit is the ultimate gift of grace.

The Holy Spirit was sent to enable us to live a naturally supernatural life. In Job 33:4, it says the Spirit of God has made

---

1 If you're not familiar with him, Watchman Nee became a Christian in Mainland China in 1920 at the age of seventeen and began writing the same year. Throughout the nearly thirty years of his ministry, Nee's life and ministry were a unique gift from the Lord to the Body of Christ. In 1952 he was imprisoned for his faith; he remained in prison until his death in 1972. His many books and writings remain an abundant source of spiritual revelation to Christians throughout the world.

me, and the breath of the Almighty has given me life. Just as the birth of a baby is a natural miracle, then our spiritual birth at salvation is a supernatural miracle.

The Holy Spirit pours out an abundance of God's love into our hearts. He helps us know God as our Father, making His love real to us. He reminds us that we are God's children, and nothing will change that, even our weaknesses and failures (see Romans 5:1-5 and Romans 8:16).

But in order to have the Holy Spirit living in us, we must be born from above. Jesus must come live in our heart because the Holy Spirit is the Spirit of Jesus. Even though we receive the Holy Spirit at our new birth, we can ask for more of Him. It's important to remember to call on Him for help because we need to be continually filled with the Spirit.

The following spiritual exercise, which will be at the end of each lesson, is to help you develop a deeper understanding of grace and better ear for hearing the voice of the Holy Spirit.

God Moment

Close your eyes and picture this: Grace is a river flowing from the throne of God. Come and stand and let Him wash you in pure water, cleansing your feet and your hands from the dust of the world.

Grace is the blood and water that flowed from Jesus' side. Lie at His feet and let the blood and water bring you freedom from all insecurities and fears. (1 Corinthians 15:10)

Grace comes out of being overshadowed by the Holy Spirit. He wants to spread His cloak over you. Grace is a well of living water in the desert in the midst of an oasis.

This is a place of rest prepared for you. Take a moment, drink, and ask the Holy Spirit to speak to you.

Revelation 7:17, 22:1; John 19:34; Exodus 17:6; Luke 1:35

Assignment:

1. *Describe a time in your life when you received undeserved favor.*

2. *Is it hard for you to receive and extend grace?*

3. *If your answer is yes, why do you think that is?*

Final thought:

The important truth from this lesson is to know that we don't have to earn God's favor because we already have all we need through Christ.

Journal:

_____

_____

_____

_____

_____

_____

_____

_____

_____

_____

_____

_____

_____

_____

_____

_____

_____

_____

_____

_____

_____

_____

_____

_____

_____

_____

_____

_____

_____

Journal:

Lesson 2: Transformed by Grace

In Genesis 1:2, the Spirit is seen actively engaged in the work of creation. He was over the earth. At the birth of Jesus, Mary was told *the Holy Spirit will come upon you, and the power of the Highest will overshadow you; therefore also, that Holy One who is to be born will be called the Son of God.* Luke 1: 34-35 states that the Holy Spirit "overshadowed" Mary, and Jesus was formed in her womb. The Holy Spirit was exerting creative energy in the womb of Mary.

Because of this, Jesus had no sin nature.

The spotless Blood of Jesus made peace for us with God, taking away our guilt. Therefore, we should not have a sin consciousness (Colossians 1:20). Sin consciousness is living under condemnation thinking you have to be and do better.

Read and summarize Hebrews 10.

_____

_____

_____

The Old Covenant sacrifices covered sin and had to be offered repeatedly. While man's sinful nature still exists, the New Covenant sacrifice of the Blood of Jesus cleanses us, and our sin is *removed* (1 John 1:7). As a result, we receive a new nature. Now when we sin, we confess and repent. If we receive a true revelation and understanding of grace, we won't live under condemnation because we will know without a doubt that when we confess and repent, we are forgiven.

Read Hebrews 9:12, 23, 28.

Condemnation brings feelings of hopelessness and despair with a sense of guilt and shame for what we have done. It is a constant weight; we keep thinking that God is disappointed in us and blaming us for messing up. On the other hand, conviction is a gentle nudge from the Holy Spirit that, yes, we messed up, but if we confess and repent, we will be forgiven, and God will not hold it against us.

With conviction, there is always hope, but with condemnation, there is only guilt.

Discussion:

Why do you think the blood of Jesus had to be taken into heaven? (Hebrews 9:11).

First comes the Blood, then the Spirit. It is because of the Blood of Jesus that we can "house" the Holy Spirit. The Blood cleanses, and the Spirit empowers because of grace. Religion works from the *outside in*, but grace works from the *inside out*. If we are living from the inside out, we should have the Holy Spirit flowing out of us. The gifts of the Spirit should be flowing out of us to others. As Christians, we are supernatural beings, but that doesn't mean we have to be super spiritual. God will use us even in our human weaknesses.

The Holy Spirit gave birth to the Church on the Day of Pentecost.

It is the Holy Spirit who is forming Christ in us. Self-effort is not going to produce anything of eternal value in us. We are empowered by grace to experience a transformation in the inner man.

The Old Testament dealt with physical acts of the outer man. The New Testament deals with the intention of the inner man and the condition of the heart. Grace and truth came through Jesus Christ. We need to learn to live internally, not externally. Man works from the outside in, but God works from the inside out. We don't find our value in rules, things, and people, but we find our value in the One who lives within us. When we live as an internal person, knowing Who lives in us, then our identity and life come from God.

When we learn to live from the inside out, the gifts of the Holy Spirit will flow out of us to others.

ⓢ *Because we have right standing in Christ, we have automatically become supernatural, but it doesn't require being super spiritual.*

It's easy to be in awe of those who prophesy or have other supernatural gifts operating through them, but they are just normal people. Being able to operate in supernatural gifts is not a sign of holiness or even character. The fact that they are called gifts means just that. They are gifts — free — not earned by how good, spiritual, or perfect someone is. Matthew 7:15-16: *we will know them by their fruit* (not by their gifts). Gifts are given, and fruit is grown; both are a result of grace.

Romans 11:29 also says the gifts and callings of God are irrevocable. Sometimes it's hard to understand why God is still using someone who has questionable character. The fruit is missing in his or her life in every area, yet the gift of God is still in them. The gifts are not flowing out of pure vessels, in fact, they rarely do. And often, if the pipes are clogged, what comes out is not pure. You can tell when something isn't quite right. A public example might be a pastor who admits to adultery, being homosexual, or misusing ministry funds in a grand way for personal gain.

The gift and calling didn't leave, but the expression of it can become warped through pride and disobedience. Eventually the sin will be exposed, and the gift will not be coming through the Spirit of God but out of the person's spirit in a carnal way.

We may have particular gifts and a specific call of God on our lives, but we still have to be obedient. When we allow fear or circumstances to cause us to disobey, we quench the Spirit. Eventually, that still small voice will be very faint, or He will stop speaking to us altogether.

Our main responsibility is simply obedience.

When we are operating in our gifting and calling, we must guard our hearts and not begin to be prideful. It's important to remember that our gifts and callings are through grace, not our own natural ability. Pride will open us up to being deceived, and, as a result, we will begin making mistakes in ministry.

Discussion:

What keeps you from obeying God when you think He is asking you to do something, especially outside your comfort zone?

Without love, our expressions of the gifts will be like a clanging cymbal, which is not a very appealing sound. The Holy Spirit is more interested in our character, the inner person of the heart, rather than how we exhibit gifts.

For example, Saul was called and anointed by God to be King. The Spirit of God came upon him, and he was turned into another man and prophesied. As time went on, however, he was disobedient, prideful, insecure, and had no relationship with God. He didn't know or trust God, therefore, he didn't understand it was grace that allowed him to rule.

To avoid his calling, he hid from God in the lost luggage (1 Samuel 10:21-22). Are you are a king in hiding, called to rule and reign, but hiding behind your baggage? (This is where we probably get the term "baggage" when referencing the things that stop us in life.)

For most of my life in ministry, I hid from the gift of teaching. My baggage was insecurity and believing lies, but when I confessed and repented, the Lord downloaded this teaching series to me. These six workbooks are the result.

King Saul was not motivated by love to serve God or others. He is a picture of what happens when you try to live out your calling through natural ability and not the power of the Holy Spirit. That is the big difference between King Saul and his successor, King David.

Prayer: *Lord, help me to remember that my success in life is not because I was born with natural abilities, it is because I can tap into your supernatural abilities. I trust You will take what I have naturally and use it supernaturally for Your glory. Amen.*

Unlike Saul, God wants us to hear Him for ourselves and not depend on someone else to tell us what He requires of us. We need to develop our own listening ear through a personal relationship with God.

Love should be the foundation for everything we do. Without it, power can lead to pride and self-inflation. Love is the greatest manifestation of God's power and is filled with truth. Love, the fruit of the Spirit that encompasses all the other fruit, is the ultimate spiritual weapon against sin, temptation, offense, etc. When we care more about others than ourselves, we will be willing to take a risk.

♥ *Love moves us outside ourselves.*

Without the working of the Holy Spirit in our hearts, it would be almost impossible to abide in love and experience joy. The fruit and the gifts go together. The gifts are not effective without fruit in your life.

In Matthew 7:20, Jesus says, by their fruit, you will know them. The Holy Spirit produces the fruit of the Christian life. Galatians 5:22, 23 shows a cluster of fruits developed in our lives through grace. The Holy Spirit wants to produce these fruits in our lives. We can't will ourselves to grow fruit. It is like putting artificial flowers in your garden. From a distance, they look good, but when you get close, there is no life or fragrance.

John 15:8-11: *by this my Father is glorified, that you bear much fruit, and so prove to be my disciples. As the Father has loved me, so have I loved you; abide in my love. If you keep my commandments, you will abide in my love, just as I have kept my Father's commandments and abide in his love. These things I have spoken to you, that my joy may be in you, and that your joy may be full.*

Allowing the fruit of the Holy Spirit to be developed in me is a choice that is mine to make, but the power to develop the fruit in my life is from the Holy Spirit.

God Moment

Ask the Holy Spirit for a revelation of grace.

Living in My grace is like living on a cruise ship in the midst of the ocean. This ship named Grace was designed with you in mind. It carries you along by a Power you can't see, but you can feel. You can rest and enjoy the benefits without the struggle to make it happen yourself. You trust the Captain knows what He is doing. You have faith He will deliver you safely. You can't see Him, but you still trust Him to be in control.

You have special privileges while living on the ship. But if you haven't discovered what they are, you won't get to enjoy them. All you have to do is ask. Take a moment and ask what your special privileges are.

I invite you to set aside time with Me, and I will share some exciting things with you. You will leave refreshed and full of joy.

You didn't earn or win your ticket because Jesus purchased it for you. It is a free gift.

Psalms 16:11

Assignment:

1. Describe a time when you tried to do something in your own strength and failed.

2. How do you think it would have turned out if you had depended on the Holy Spirit to accomplish the task?

3. How have you felt about people who didn't seem to be living the way you thought they should, yet God was using them anyway?

4. Consider using this chart as you think through major relationships in your life when you judged people for their behavior. Look back and try to see how God used the situation to teach you something.

Person	Situation	Feeling	Judgment

We extend grace when we don't judge others regardless of their behavior and how they make us feel.

Prayer: *Father, I choose to forgive_____ for their behavior and how it made me feel. I release them to You to be all that You created them to be. Help me see them through Your eyes.*

Ask the Lord to show you His heart toward them and their heart toward Him. Then, ask Him to bless them in spite of their behavior. Journal what the Holy Spirit tells you about grace and self-effort.

Final thought:

We need a revelation that our results and abilities are rooted in our dependence on Him.

Journal:

_____

_____

_____

_____

_____

_____

_____

_____

_____

_____

_____

_____

_____

_____

_____

_____

_____

_____

_____

_____

_____

_____

_____

_____

_____

_____

_____

_____

_____

_____

_____

Journal:

_____

_____

_____

_____

_____

_____

_____

_____

_____

_____

_____

_____

_____

_____

_____

_____

_____

_____

_____

_____

_____

_____

_____

_____

_____

_____

_____

_____

_____

Lesson 3: Bearing Fruit through Grace

When examining the fruit of the Spirit in scripture, we see that there are three groups or clusters of fruit:

• The first group is in relation to God: love, joy, and peace. Romans 5:5: *The love of God has been poured out in our hearts by the Holy Spirit who was given to us.* It's important to ask the Lord to show us how to love Him with our whole being, and to love others as ourselves and be filled with His joy from within while we abide in peace (Romans 5:5).

• The second group is in relation to other people: our attitude toward others should be one of longsuffering, gentleness, and goodness.

• The third group is for our individual Christian life: we need to develop a life of faith, meekness, and self-control in our personal lives.

Like Esther, we are being prepared as a Bride for Christ. When we have been in the presence of the King, we will look and smell different. All fruit of the Spirit flows out of love. How we relate to God, others, and how we live out our faith will look different when we respond in love.

When the love of God is apparent in us and flows through us, we will exhibit all the other fruit, which are the characteristics of the love of Christ.

1 Peter 4:14: *the Spirit of glory and of God rests upon you.*

What is glory? Glory is used here to mean the character of God. The Holy Spirit is the one who produces God-like character in believers. Talk about unmerited favor! That is pure grace.

2 Corinthians 3:18 reinforces that by telling us that we are all being transformed daily as we abide in Him.

The Holy Spirit wants to build character in us and help us grow fruit.

In his booklet, *The Key to Everything*, missionary, author, and evangelist, Norman Grubb, makes an insightful point. In the teaching on the vine and the branches, with God as the vine, we, as the branches, are brought into living relationship with our Father God and can draw on the "sap" of His Kingdom life (John 15:1-11). Abiding in this "oneness," we can produce the leaves, flowers, and fruit He has ordained for us. Grubb underscores that the *activity* of the branch is secondary to its *receptivity*. "We fail when we make activity a substitute for receptivity. He is the Lord and we are the co-operators, the receivers."

Only in this relationship with Him can we become the true givers of His life, beauty, and light. Then we become, as in Elizabeth Barrett Browning's famed verse, "...a common bush aflame with the Presence of God."

When we make activity a substitute for receptivity, we are living under the law.

Legalism brings frustration and quenches the Spirit. We discount grace when we try to earn a place of favor with God or man. When we understand that it's by grace we receive all God has to give, we then draw near to Jesus and allow His presence to bring forth life. Romans 8:11 reminds us that just as the

Holy Spirit raised Jesus from the dead, that same Spirit lives in us and has raised us from death.

Until the Holy Spirit fell on the believers at Pentecost, they did not have power to be a witness for Christ. Peter is an example when he denied Jesus three times before the resurrection but could preach boldly with no fear after he was filled with the Spirit.

There were 120 priests sounding trumpets when Solomon finished the temple (2 Chronicles 5:12), and there were 120 people in the upper room on the Day of Pentecost when the Holy Spirit descended. The trumpets in Solomon's day announced the completion of the temple. On the Day of Pentecost, the Holy Spirit announced the completion of another temple. It was a temple of believers who were now filled with the Holy Spirit. After the sound of a mighty wind, the glory of the Lord filled the upper room. It marked the beginning of the Age of the Spirit.

That means we also begin to live in the Age of the Holy Spirit when we are born again. The work of the Holy Spirit is to constantly bear witness of Jesus and His finished work to the world. He does this largely through us as believers. Acts 1:5-8 tells us that the Holy Spirit will give us power to be a witness.

Discussion:

What are some ways we should be witnesses?

For this reason, we should be interested in experiencing all Christ has for us through the ministry of the Holy Spirit. All gifts are meant to flow from grace and love through us to others. They come out of a heart of compassion. The gifts we receive from the Spirit flow from unmerited favor not only for us but also for others to receive through us. We are meant to be a conduit for God's grace, love, and mercy.

Spiritual gifts are distributed among believers according to the will of the Spirit (1 Corinthians 12:1).

The Holy Spirit came to give us understanding.

Now we have received not the spirit of the world, but the Spirit who is from God, that we might understand the things freely given us by God (1 Corinthians 2:12).

We live a supernatural life because the Holy Spirit lives in us.

There is a great misconception that we have to be good enough for God to use us as a blessing to others. In the *Discipline of Grace,* Jerry Bridges says, "How good is good enough?" We need to be clean vessels but also recognize that we are imperfect. He also says, "Your worst days are never so bad that you are beyond the reach of God's grace. And your best days are never so good that you are beyond the need of God's grace."

The Greek word for the gifts of the Spirit is *charisma,* which *Strong's Concordance* defines as "gifts of grace, a favor which one receives without any merit of his own."

In 1 Corinthians 1: 4-7, the word *gift* is charisma. *Charis* is grace or underserved favor, spiritual endowment, or divine favor. Everything we do should be anchored in grace. To give grace, we have to receive grace, which means not living under the bondage of performance and legalism.

Legalism is trying to perform in a certain way to gain favor with God. We don't have to earn favor with God; we already have all the favor we need because we do not live under the Old Testament Law of performance; we live in a new era of New

Testament grace, which is a gift. (We will go into more about grace vs. legalism in Workbook 4, *Spiritual Warfare*.)

Within the Trinity, each person of the Godhead performs a different role.

• Everything originates with God; He **gives** the command.

• Jesus is the legal authority; He **administrates** and **performs** the command.

• The Holy Spirit **brings the manifestation.**

One of my teachers once used this example: "If I ask you to turn on the light, there are three forces involved. First, I **give** the command; second, you walk over and turn on the light — so you **administrate,** or **perform** the command. But finally, who brings on the light? It is not either of us. It is the **power** — the electricity, that produces the light and brings the **manifestation.**" When God said, "Let there be light," it was the Son who performed it, and then the Holy Spirit brought it forth.

⊘ **The Holy Spirit is the power, yet He is also a person.**

His light shines in our hearts to light up the darkness around us. We have been set apart to be different from the world. We reflect the face of Christ when we glorify God by allowing the Holy Spirit to bring about the manifestation of His power.

2 Corinthians 4: 6-7: *we are jars of clay showing that the surpassing power belongs to God and not to us.*

God will use us in our humanity.

One Lord, One Faith, and One Baptism (1 Corinthians 12:13). This one baptism is referring to when the Holy Spirit baptizes us into the Body of Christ as a new believer, which only happens once. There are other kinds of baptisms, covered in lesson 8. However, we are told in Matthew 3:11, Mark 1:8, Luke 3:16, and John 1:33-34, that Jesus baptizes us with the Holy Spirit.

This fulfills a promise from the Old Testament. Back then, God poured out His Spirit only on certain people to accomplish a specific task. But Joel 2:28-29 promised that God would pour out His Spirit on *all* His people—male and female, young and old. He does this through Jesus and the Holy Spirit. After you are born again, you have the Holy Spirit living in you, and you now have access to the gifts of the Spirit.

If you have never accepted Christ as your Savior pray this prayer:

Lord, I confess that I am a sinner and need to be saved by your grace. I repent of my sins and renounce all my sinful ways. I ask you to come into my heart and cleanse me. I thank you for the gift of the Holy Spirit and ask you to fill me to overflowing and empower me to live the life you have for me. Thank you, Lord Jesus, for giving me a new identity. Amen.

Be sure to tell someone that you have become a new creature in Christ. Begin to read your Bible starting with the book of John in the New Testament and ask the Lord to give you the boldness the apostles had. Even if you have been a believer for many years, ask the Lord to give you all He has for you to do the work He wants you to accomplish. Most of us need more boldness to influence those around us.

God Moment

Ask God to bring you into this kind of rest.

Living in the will of God and laboring with Him is like being in the Garden of Eden, where the ground gave forth a mist that watered the earth.

My Spirit rises up from deep within you like a well of living water that brings life to you and those around you.

Living like the world lives is like being in the midst of a storm all the time. It's mostly turmoil and striving. Beloved, you are to be as a well-watered garden with new life springing up around you. You have in your heart living water to offer because you have been restored to the Garden, to My Sabbath rest. So go to the well of living water and ask Me for a drink. I am waiting.

Beloved, when you are still and soak in My presence, it is like a gentle spring rain that brings new life. It is very restful and peaceful. Take a moment and soak.

John 4:10; 7:38; Genesis 2:6

Assignment:

1. How do you see God working in your life to develop fruit and build character?

_____

_____

2. *Describe a time in your life that you knew the Holy Spirit was empowering you to be a witness.*

_____

_____

3. *What do you think it means for you personally to live in the age of the Holy Spirit?*

_____

_____

4. *In looking at the fruit of the Spirit as "grace clusters" where do you feel the most challenged to reflect Christ? Briefly explain.*

_____

_____

5. *How have you made "activity" a substitute for "receptivity?"*

_____

_____

6. *Look up scriptures on grace and journal what the Holy Spirit shows you as you meditate on them (Zechariah 4:7, Romans 4: 16, Acts 14:26).*

_____

_____

Final thought:

You cannot, through your will, cause fruit to be grown in your life. It is a supernatural work of the Holy Spirit.

Journal:

_____

_____

_____

_____

_____

_____

_____

_____

_____

_____

_____

_____

_____

_____

_____

_____

_____

_____

_____

_____

_____

_____

_____

_____

_____

_____

_____

_____

_____

_____

_____

_____

Journal:

Section Two

Topic Two: The Gift

The gift of the Holy Spirit is to empower us to be a witness and equip us to do the works Jesus did. Freely we have received; therefore, we are supposed to freely give. Through His power, we can boldly preach the gospel, heal the sick, cast out demons, and make "disciples of all the nations."

Luke 24:49; Matthew 10:8

Lesson 4: Different Categories of Gifts

Jesus did not leave us helpless, since the Gift of the Holy Spirit was sent to us as a Helper. (John 14:26, 15:26).

Grace and spiritual gifts both have an active influence on a believer's life.

Paul said in 1 Corinthians 12:1, *"now concerning spiritual gifts, I would not have you ignorant.* At birth, God gives us natural gifts, and when we are born again, the Holy Spirit imparts spiritual gifts to us. Also, scripture tells us that Jesus himself imparts gifts to us to equip the church. The gifts are most effective when they flow out of love for God and others (Mark 12:30-31).

1 Corinthians 14:4-5 explains that when we pray in our spiritual language, we are talking to God and edifying ourselves, that is, building ourselves up. This is a good thing; it's like recharging your spiritual batteries.

Incidentally, nowhere in scripture does it say that it's a sin or blasphemous to do so, but some people act offended to hear tongues without an interpretation. Rather, it simply means that the person is talking to God, and God isn't speaking through them to anyone else.

1 Corinthians 14:16-17 tells us that when you pray in your prayer language, you are giving thanks sufficiently as an individual. However, no one but God understands what you are saying. Therefore, the church is not edified.

The Fruits of the Holy Spirit — love, joy, peace, patience, kindness, goodness, faithfulness, gentleness, and self-control — aren't particularly controversial within the church. Even if they aren't always as evident as they should be, nobody is debating their place in the believer's life. However, the Gifts of the Holy Spirit — wisdom, knowledge, faith, healing, miracles, prophecy, discerning the spirits, tongues, and interpretation of tongues — have sparked fiery debates that have often led to church splits and wounds within the Body of Christ.

Some Christian churches teach the idea of Cessationism, which is the belief that the gifts listed in 1 Corinthians 12 ceased operating after the last apostle died. The idea of Cessationism was started, in large part, by John Calvin.

Don't avoid what you don't understand.[1]

"Some of these [spiritual] gifts seem strange to those who have not encountered them in the course of their walk with Christ, and sometimes they still seem strange to those of us that have. Some examples of spiritual gifts being used in scripture leave us with questions, and many times the examples we have encountered in our lives have left even more questions. For those of us who like things clearly defined, it can be tempting to just avoid the stuff that isn't neat and tidy. But Paul reminds us that these gifts all come from the same Holy Spirit (1 Corinthians 12:11). Then he quickly tells us that the body is made of many parts that operate differently, but together.

"Just as hands, eyes, feet, and ears look and perform very differently from each other, so, too, the gifts of the Holy Spirit look and operate differently within God's church. With that in mind, it would be a mistake to completely ignore these gifts.

---

1 For more information on the spiritual gifts, their history, basis in Scripture, and why they are so controversial, see Appendix.

God gave them to the church to serve a powerful purpose, and it seems obvious the enemy would want to remove that power from church life. That's something to consider for a moment. A church that tries to operate with only part of the tools God has provided her with is a much weaker opponent.

"We need to approach this subject with hearts open to truth, while praying for discernment. Even those of us who have experienced these gifts still have much to learn. The Holy Spirit will lead and guide us in all truth if we just ask, listen, and respond." – Derek Morgan

Spiritual gifts are different from talents or natural gifts.

Talents are *natural gifts* we receive at birth. They are things we are naturally good at doing, like playing a musical instrument, painting, or singing. These are God-given and, therefore, not necessarily given to us by the Holy Spirit. When we become believers, the Holy Spirit will enhance these natural gifts as we submit them to Him to be used for the glory of God.

Spiritual gifts are supernatural manifestations of God's power provided by the Holy Spirit (1 Corinthians 12). Spiritual gifts are the direct result of the Holy Spirit's supernatural activity in a person providing him with gifts separate from any natural talent. In 1 Corinthians 2:4-5, Paul says *my message and my preaching were not with wise and persuasive words, but with a demonstration of the Spirit's power.*

Summarize 1 Corinthians 13:

_____

_____

_____

_____

_____

Let's look at gifts we see in scripture and examine how they reflect the different roles of the Godhead. There are three groups of gifts listed in scripture given by Father, Son, and Holy Spirit. Each of us has been given a gift either naturally or supernaturally.

Gifts from the Father in Romans 12:4-8 are personal gifts that come naturally from birth. They are yours. Verse 4 says *we have many members in one body, but all the members do not have the same function.* Verse 6 says *we have gifts that differ according to the grace that is given to us.* We are naturally motivated in certain ways, whether we are Christian or not. When these gifts operate through a believer, it is to the glory of God. The gifts are enhanced after we become believers, and, as believers, these motivational gifts tend to define and characterize a person's ongoing, day-to-day role of service within the Body of Christ.

Ephesians 4:8-11 says, *when He ascended on high, He led captivity captive, and gave gifts to men.* Verse 11 says, *"He Himself gave some to be apostles, some prophets, some evangelists and some pastors and teachers."*

These are gifts from Jesus to the Church for ministry to the Body. The person filling this role is not the gift; the ministry is the gift. Both the *ESV Commentary* and *Grudem's Systematic Theology* agree with the teaching that these Ephesians gifts are being listed as offices usually appointed by the leadership of the Church to equip the saints within the Body. They are the ones who maintain the vision of the church. Not everyone will function in the Body of Christ using these gifts.

Gifts from the Father, Son, and Holy Spirit:

In 1 Corinthians 12: 1-12, it says, *"spiritual gifts empower you to be a conduit for the Holy Spirit."* These gifts, which manifest through us as He wills, belong to the Holy Spirit.

Gifts of the Holy Spirit

As believers, we may experience one or more of these 1 Corinthians 12:1-11 gifts throughout our lifetimes. Some people seem to flow effortlessly into these gifts as they are developed over time. Others may experience these blessings manifesting through them as the need arises or as the Spirit wills. We do not do anything to earn them, and it doesn't indicate spiritual maturity when God uses us this way. They are gifts to those receiving healing, edification, exhortation, and comfort.

These blessings tend to be given when specific needs arise within the Church. When we exercise these gifts, the Holy Spirit is actually manifesting or expressing Himself through them. Spiritual gifts have an active influence because they are meeting needs in practical or natural *and* spiritual or super-natural ways.

Gifts from the Holy Spirit in 1 Corinthians 12 are in three categories (supernaturally gifted):

A. **Gifts of Utterance** – These *say* something.

1. Tongues — known and unknown languages inspired by the Holy Spirit.

2. Interpretation of tongues — reveal the meaning of what was spoken by the Holy Spirit, not necessarily a transliteration of what is said, but a translation.

3. Prophecy — a divine utterance spoken by faith, flowing from the Holy Spirit within a person. It's not through our mind or intellect. It is applied for exhortation, comfort, and edification. It enables one to speak with forthrightness, insight, and moral boldness. Prophecy edifies the church by encouraging and exhorting those hearing it (1 Corinthians 14:3).

B. **Gifts of Power** — These *do* something.

1. Faith — to believe without doubt, a supernatural ability to combat unbelief, an inner conviction (a "knowing in your knower").

2. Healings — to induce health without human aid or may include divinely assisted application of human instrumentation and medical means.

3. Miracles — to be a conduit for power beyond human means, bringing authority over sin, Satan, sickness, etc.

C. **Gifts of Revelation** — These reveal something.

1. Word of knowledge — supernatural knowledge download about God's divine will and revelation.

2. Discerning of spirits — the power to detect the spirit realm, which is not the same as a spirit of discernment, which can be just suspicion.

3. Words of wisdom — supernatural insight, intuition in problem solving, perspective, sense of divine direction. This gift works interactively with knowledge and discernment.

Gifts given by God

Gifts given by God are listed in Romans 12:3-8 — for basic life purpose and motivation (naturally gifted); these gifts are enhanced in believers.

1. Prophecy/Perceiver — Perceivers should bring exhortation, comfort, and edification to others. They have a very intuitive sense of knowing what is happening in the natural and or spirit realm.

2. Ministry/Service — loving, general service to meet the needs of others.

3. Teaching — instructs, informs, and educates, especially as a profession.

4. Exhortation — to entreat, comfort, or exhort.

5. Giving — generosity or liberal giving.

6. Leadership/Administration — organizer and "upfront" person.

7. Mercy — feels sympathy with misery of another and relates to others in empathy, respect, and honesty.

Gifts given from the Son

The gifts from the Son are listed in Ephesians 4:11-13 and are given to facilitate and equip the Body (supernaturally natural).

1. Apostle — start works, oversee large sections of Body, and hold broader leadership roles.

2. Prophet — spiritually mature spokesperson with divinely focused message to the Body at large and uniquely gifted for future events (preacher/teacher).

3. Evangelist — has a special gift of preaching or witnessing that brings salvation to the lost; missions focus.

4. Pastor — "protect" and shepherd the people, nurtures, and cares for spiritual needs, either one-on-one or *en masse*.

5. Teacher — supernatural ability to explain and apply truths received from God for the Body of believers and is insightful and effective in conveying concepts.

Discussion:

Where are you in your understanding about the role of the Trinity in imparting these gifts?

These positions in the church are meeting needs that are both natural (practical) and supernatural (spiritual). Spiritual gifts allow the Holy Spirit to manifest and express Himself supernaturally to His people and through His people in a naturally supernatural way.

The grace from Christ Jesus, which is sent by the love of God, brings us into fellowship with the Holy Spirit, who is the Gift to the Church. We cannot be in touch with the Father and Son without the Holy Spirit **(Ephesians 2:18-22)**.

Prayer: *Lord, I'm asking for this kind of infilling of the Spirit. I want to experience all you have for me. I'm asking for spiritual gifts to flow through me to others. Show me which gifts you want me to have. Amen.*

God Moment

After reflecting on the truths below, ask for more of God's grace to flow through you to others.

Beloved, when you walk in love while living in this world, you will experience the gentle rain and be challenged by the storms of life, but there will be peace in the midst of the storms. Just quiet your soul and let Me be your shelter.

Then you will be like a garden where people can come and be watered, fed, and then blossom into all I have destined them to be. You will be like a well-watered vine that goes beyond your walls and reaches out to their world.

I will give you the wisdom, discernment, and understanding about how to love others as you love Me. They are the helpless and hurting. Some are wounded warriors walking in a daze, wondering what happened to them. They thought they were doing it right. They need an oasis.

Are you one of those, dear one? First, you need to love yourself. You have all you need: grace. Take a moment and draw from the well. There is enough for everyone.

Zechariah 4:6-7

Song of Solomon 4:16

Assignment:

1. If you grew up in a legalistic home where your acceptance had to do with how well you kept the rules or performed, how would that affect your ability to receive and understand grace?

_____

_____

2. If we really grasped grace, would we hesitate to pray for someone's healing?

_____

_____

3. How would your Christian walk be different if you relied on God's grace and the power of the Holy Spirit to operate in your life?

_____

_____

4. *How would that change the way you approach sharing the gospel?*

_____

_____

5. *Do you really believe those gifts are freely given, or do you tend to think you have to earn them?*

_____

_____

6. *Where does your thinking about the gifts come from?*

_____

_____

Final thought:

You don't have to be good enough or super-spiritual for God to impart spiritual gifts to you. Remember that gifts are given, and fruit is grown but not from self-effort. Grace freely given to us in Christ Jesus enables us to live a supernatural life naturally by walking in the power of the Holy Spirit. Grace empowers us beyond our ability. It takes the pressure off.

Lesson 5: The Gift of the Holy Spirit

When we are born again, we receive the Holy Spirit Himself.

The Work of the Holy Spirit:

The work of the Holy Spirit is to manifest the active presence of God in the world and especially in the Church. Every Christian receives the Holy Spirit at conversion, which is confirmed in 1 Corinthians 12:13; Ephesians 1:13.

Subsequent to conversion, it is essential for every believer to thirst for fresh encounters with the person of the Holy Spirit John 7:37-39. The Holy Spirit performs many necessary ministries in the believer's life such as Counselor (John 14:16), Teacher (John 14: 26), Revealer of Jesus Christ as Lord (1 Corinthians 12:3), Empowerer (Acts 1:8), Guide (Romans 8:14), Intercessor (Romans 8:26-27), Giver of Spiritual Gifts (1 Corinthians 12:11; 1 Corinthians 14), the One who brings conviction (John 16:8; Acts 7:51), and produces spiritual fruit (Galatians 5:22-25) and spiritual passion (Luke 3:16).

In the Old Testament, we don't see the Holy Spirit mentioned by name, but we see His ministry as a servant in action. We see Him as a servant introducing Ruth and Boaz and finding a bride for Isaac. These examples are a picture of the Holy Spirit finding and preparing us as a bride for Christ today. See Ruth 2:5; Genesis 24:2; Revelation 19:7, 21:9.

God's Spirit is like a guarantee or pledge that confirms God's love for us and assures us that His promises are true. We receive His Spirit when we first accept Jesus into our hearts. His Spirit unites with our spirit, giving us a brand-new source of life, energy, and power. It's the Spirit of God that bears witness or validates to our spirit, not only that we are His children, but also that He loves us (Romans 8:10). It's God's Spirit that empowers, teaches, counsels, convicts, reveals Christ, intercedes, guides, gives us discernment in our walk, and enables us to commune and fellowship with Him. The Holy Spirit was sent as a Helper. Jesus did not leave us helpless after He ascended into heaven (John 14:26, 15:26).

The gift of the Holy Spirit is given to us at the new birth.

Jesus ascended so the Holy Spirit could descend.

The Holy Spirit is the ultimate gift to the church, empowering us to live life naturally in the supernatural. Romans 8:2: *for the law of the Spirit of life in Christ Jesus has made me free from the law of sin and death.* The Spirit is the dynamic of a believer's experience that leads them into liberty and empowers them to live the Christ life.

Acts 10:38: *God anointed Jesus of Nazareth with the Holy Spirit and with power: who went about doing good.* If Jesus needed to be anointed with the Holy Spirit and power for His ministry, how much more do we need anointing and empowerment?

The New Testament is in the Old Testament concealed; the Old Testament is in the New Testament revealed.

When we read the Old Testament, we can look for "types and shadows" in the New Testament, revealed through the stories and lives of the people. Their lives and challenges are natural examples of spiritual truth for us who strive to live empowered by the Holy Spirit. Some are a picture of faith (or lack of it), others of failure; others show moral weakness. Even though we see sin patterns in the lives of some, God used them anyway when their hearts were repentant.

The New Testament addresses the same problems in us, yet God will use us anyway if we ask for forgiveness.

Discussion:

What do you struggle with the most in your relationship with others and God?

The book of Ezekiel is a world of imagination, rich in symbolism and visualization. We see the Holy Spirit as both the power source and the energy source in Ezekiel 1. Ezekiel means "*God strengthens.*"

Ezekiel was a priest and prophet, probably from the same tribe as Zadok. (Zadok was the priest who remained loyal to David and then anointed Solomon as king.) In Ezekiel 2:2, he had a unique experience of the Spirit entering him and empowering him to be a witness. Ezekiel was deported to Babylon when he was about twenty-five years old. (The current location of Babylon is Iraq, about fifty-five miles south of Baghdad.) He was probably about thirty years old when he had the first vision in Ezekiel 1 and about fifty years old when he had the last one recorded. This is significant because 20 years was the same length of time a priest served in the Tabernacle and in the Temple.

The kingdom of Israel was divided when Solomon's son Rehoboam took over the rule as king, and he refused to lower the oppressive tax rate his father had imposed upon the people. He listened to his young friends instead of older and wiser advisors. So, this gave his brother Jeroboam the opportunity to lead a rebellion. Ezekiel was a prophet and priest to the southern kingdom of Judah.

Christian author, Chuck Missler, in teaching about Jeroboam, said, "Jeroboam probably knew the religious center would always tug at the hearts of the people, so it was good politics to try to break Jerusalem's emotional hold over the people." So, Jeroboam set up two centers for idol worship, Dan in the north and Bethel in the south, which caused the nation to split in two.

The northern kingdom under Jeroboam went into idolatry. They called themselves the "House of Israel." The northern capitol was Samaria. (In Jesus' day, the Jews despised Samaritans as a people of mixed heredity with a polluted religion.)

The southern kingdom under Rehoboam still maintained Jerusalem as its capitol and was called the "House of Judah." However, both the tribes of Benjamin and Simeon had become enmeshed with this "House." Also, the faithful "remnant from all the tribes in the north migrated to the south where Temple worship was the "politically correct" thing to do. (They either had a pure heart for the One True God, or they were just keeping rules by performing rituals.) It is interesting that this idolatry was taking place in the north since Satan said he would "sit on the mount of the congregation on the farthest sides of the north" (Isaiah 14:13).

Just as he did with the Israelites, Satan will tempt us to set up idols in our hearts, which will cause us to be divided in our devotion to the One True God.

Prayer: *Lord, show me the idols that reign in my heart. I repent for looking to anyone or anything other than You to meet my needs. I repent for trying to gain fulfillment, recognition, power, or praise from anyone but You. I ask You to be Lord of my heart and mind in every area. Amen.*

Discussion:

What are some of the idols we tend to have in our lives?

Some of the most vivid symbolism of the Holy Spirit is in Ezekiel 1 and 2:1-2. Ezekiel saw a whirlwind bringing four living creatures with four faces called cherubim. The faces were:

- A Lion representing sovereignty and supremacy.

- An Ox representing humility, service, and sacrifice.

- A Man representing the intellect and understanding with insights into life.

- An Eagle representing deity with heavenly, divine perspective.

These four faces are also seen reflected in the four Gospels. (Matthew portrays Jesus as lion, Mark portrays Him as an ox, Luke portrays Jesus as a man, and John portrays Him as the eagle.) They reflect the nature and character of Christ. The Lord wants to use the Holy Spirit to transform us into the image of Christ. As we reflect His nature and character, we glorify God.

In Ezekiel 1:16, we also see a picture of the activity of God portrayed in "the wheel in the middle of a wheel." We can look at this symbolically as the Spirit of God within our spirit taking us where He wants us to go. A wheel represents eternity because it has no beginning and no end.

The Holy Spirit is eternal, and so is the human spirit. After the new birth, the Holy Spirit is within us. As believers, the Spirit within our spirit should be taking us wherever the Lord wants us to go. As in verse 12, we should not turn aside from doing what seems impossible. When He says go, we go; when He says stay, we stay.

Discussion:

What would keep you from asking God to take you where He wants you to go? Describe how you would go about allowing the Holy Spirit to lead you.

Sometimes we have to break religious mindsets in order to be led by the Spirit. It might require repenting of prejudicial mindsets and crucifying our flesh. The wall standing between us and the blessings God has for us needs to come down. Where

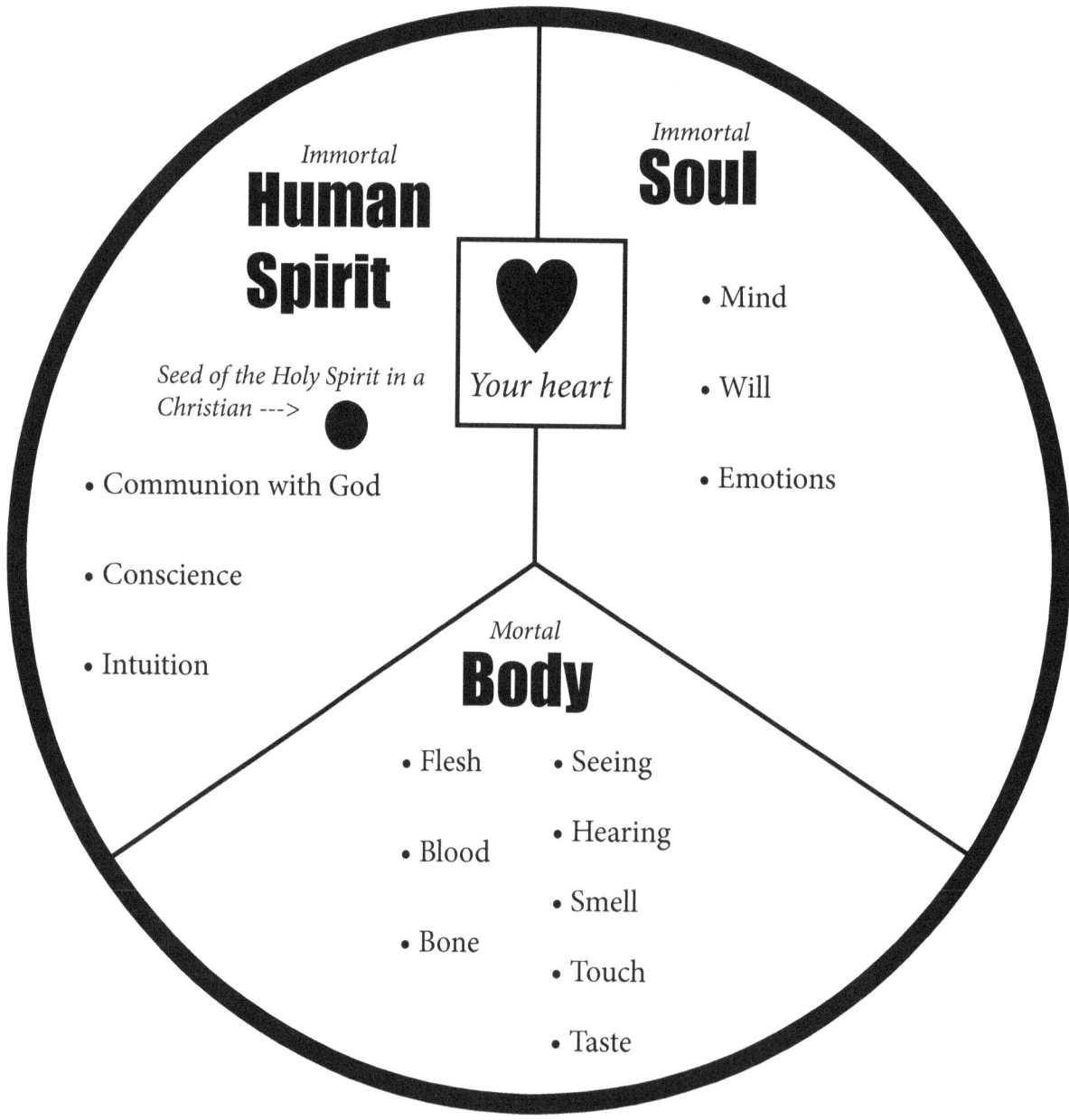

Immortal
Human Spirit

Seed of the Holy Spirit in a Christian --->

Your heart

• Communion with God

• Conscience

• Intuition

Immortal
Soul

• Mind

• Will

• Emotions

Mortal
Body

• Flesh   • Seeing

• Blood   • Hearing

• Bone   • Smell

• Touch

• Taste

God wants to lead may not be where we thought we could go. To be led by the Spirit requires faith, humility, and surrender to whatever He has for us. *Thy will be done, not mine.*

Cherubim Illustration by Drew Pryor, 16 years old, 2014

Assuming the Cherubim reflect the nature and character of God, then perhaps this is how the Holy Spirit works within us to form us into the image of Christ. He takes our humanity and transforms us into servants who become lions, ruling and reigning with Christ with heavenly vision like the eagle.

Prayer: *Lord, I give You permission to take me wherever You want me to go. Help me to trust You completely. I surrender my will to Yours. Amen.*

Mark 8:34: *"Summoning the crowd along with His disciples, He said to them, 'If anyone wants to be my disciple, he must deny himself, take up his cross, and follow me'."*

God Moment

Ask the Lord to help you bask in the light of His presence.

Take a moment and feel the warm glow of My presence on your face. Smell the soft alluring fragrance? Do you glimpse a light peeking over the top of the hill? Step out and walk toward that light. It's Me, Jesus, coming down the hill toward you.

Beloved, I am the radiance of my Father's glory, and I want to shine through you. I want to bring you to a field of flowers on the hillside lit with the light of My glory. I want to set you free to be like a little child in My presence. See yourself dancing, laughing, playing, and running with your arms stretched out. Turn your face upward to embrace and welcome My light. Take a moment and dance.

When you come into my presence with abandonment, you will go out filled with love and acceptance. But I want you to come full circle. I want you to go out and take some of the flowers to others. After you share the fragrance, come back and get some more.

Beloved, pick another bouquet and offer it back to Me. When you do, the flowers will become all the faces you are praying for. Take My hand; walk with Me, and together we will bring them up the hill toward the light.

2 Corinthians 2:14-15

Isaiah 60:1-5

Revelation 21:23

Assignment:

1. Describe a time when you felt God was directing you to go and do something.

_____

_____

2. How have your weaknesses kept you from being used by God to minister to others?

_____

_____

3. If God has ever taken you outside your comfort zone and caused you to be wholly dependent on the Holy Spirit, describe what that involved.

_____

_____

4. Which of the faces on the cherubim do you feel reflect you the most, and how does that look in your life?

_____

_____

5. Write down the names of the faces on the flowers and ask the Lord how He feels about each of them. Be still and listen so you can journal what you sense He is saying to you.

_____

_____

Final thought:

God wants us to live supernaturally, connected to His power source
— the Holy Spirit.

Journal:

Lesson 6: Transformation

We see the four faces of the Cherubim in Ezekiel again on four of the tribal standards of Israel.

When Israel camped in the wilderness around the Tabernacle, four tribal standards were raised. These give us a glimpse of the nature and character of Jesus in the Old Testament. Each had its symbol on them for all to see (Numbers 2:2-25, 10:14-25).

They were:

- Judah's standard was the Lion, and they camped on the East side

- Ephraim's standard was the Ox, and they camped on the West side

- Reuben's standard was the Man, and they camped on the South side

- Dan's standard was the Eagle, and they camped on the North side

We also see these four faces reflecting the nature and character of Jesus in the gospels:

- *Matthew* was written to the *Jews* and represents Jesus as the Lion of the tribe of *Judah*

- *Mark* was written to the *Romans* and represents Christ as the servant *Ox*

- *Luke* was written to the *Gentiles* and represents Jesus as the Son of *Man*

- *John* was written to the *Church* and represents Jesus as the *Son of God*, the *Eagle*

The tribes of Israel were instructed to camp around the tabernacle to the north, south, east, and west by groups of three tribes each: three in the north, three in the east, three in the west, and the largest three tribes in the south (Numbers 1:1-43).

In each group of three tribes, one tribe was recognized as that group's leader. Each of them had its own standard or banner identifying it as a tribal head, while the other tribes had a lesser type of banner. The tribal heads' standards were larger and each displayed one of the four faces we see on the cherubim, thereby making a statement to the spirit realm.

The placement of their camps was important because when Balak tried to have Balaam curse Israel as they looked down from the mountain, they saw the encampment, which formed the shape of a cross. This is a conclusion determined by the number of people and tents in each tribe.

God would not allow Balaam to curse them so Balaam told Balak how to entice them to sin, which would then open the door for curses to come upon them. It is the same for us; the enemy cannot cause a curse to come on us unless we open the door through sin (Proverbs 26:2). Because we are in Christ, the cross sets us free from the curse of the Law. We are protected by the Blood of Jesus.

Galatians 3:13: *Christ has redeemed us from the curse of the law, being made a curse for us: for cursed is everyone who is hanged on a tree, so that in Christ Jesus the blessings of Abraham might come on the Gentiles, so that we might receive the promise of the Holy Spirit through faith. (ESV)*

We have an advocate in Christ, and we are under His protection. The priests were camped between the Israelites and the Tent of Meeting, so they were in the midst of the people as intercessors. Likewise, Jesus is our High Priest and intercessor (Hebrews 4:14).

However, when we give in to sin's temptation and willingly sin, God removes His protection. So, in effect, when we sin, we open the door to the enemy.

Balaam took advantage of this principle when he told Balak how to bring them out from under God's protection by using the women to tempt and trap them in sexual sin, which led to the Israelites following the women into the worship of their gods. Hence, they brought a curse on themselves (Revelation 2:14).

Discussion:

What does that mean for us when we think of Jesus as a buffer making intercession for us with God?

Isaiah 59:19: so shall they fear the name of the Lord from the west, and His glory from the rising of the sun. When the enemy shall come in like a flood, the Spirit of the Lord shall lift up a standard against him.

The faces on these tribal leaders' standards are first seen on the four creatures in the whirlwind in Ezekiel 1:10. This scene reminds us of when the Holy Spirit came on the day of Pentecost. Acts 2:2: *and suddenly there came a sound from heaven as of a rushing, mighty wind.* The Holy Spirit came to transform us spiritually from the inside out into the nature of Christ.

I believe the four faces of the cherubim represent the character and glory that the Spirit of the Lord is transforming us into daily. The Holy Spirit came to develop His character in us so we can bear fruit. He has made us partakers of His divine nature, which happens as we follow the leading of the Holy Spirit.

The following story is a good example of being supernaturally led by the Spirit and not by the natural reasoning of your mind:

"Fanatic in the Attic, Feller in the Cellar"

Author Arthur Burk, who lived in Wales, taught us a lot about learning to hear from God. He taught us about the "fanatic in the attic" which represents your spirit, and the "feller in the cellar" representing your mind. The fanatic in the attic can see a long way off, and he can see around corners — there's no distance or time in the spirit realm. The feller in the cellar can only see what's right in front of him because he doesn't operate in the realm of faith.

Arthur tells of one very cold and rainy Sunday afternoon in England years ago when he was riding on a bus in the English countryside, going between two towns.

Suddenly, the fanatic in the attic spoke to him: *"Arthur, get off the bus at the next stop."* Arthur looked out of the bus. Rain, cold rain, and there was *nothing*. At that point, the Fanatic and Feller inside his head started arguing about the wisdom of taking action, but the next stop was coming up, and Arthur had to decide "who" to listen to...

It's a great and personal story Burk tells on himself, but I don't want you to miss the point.

We Have to Make the Choice

We have choices all the time, because, to use Burk's analogy, your spirit man (the fanatic in the attic) and your mind (the feller in the cellar) both talk to you all the time. The Holy Spirit is always telling you to step out in faith, sometimes even giving instructions that make no sense to the mind. You and I have to choose, just like Arthur on the bus. The directions we get often leave us feeling foolish, uncertain, or both. Yet we must choose to act or ignore.

To finish the story: "*Arthur jumped up and rang the little bell that tells the bus to stop. Shortly after that, the bus came to a halt and Arthur got off. The bus pulled away and Arthur was left standing alone in the rain. Nothing in sight — not even a house. He stood there, alone, in the rain, getting cold. The fella in the cellar spoke up, 'Well, what now? I told you, you would be stuck'.*

"*But there was nowhere to go, so he stood there — getting wetter and colder, of course. After about 10 minutes, a car drove by — and then suddenly screeched to a halt and started to reverse back toward Arthur. The windows rolled down and several heads popped out of the windows. 'Arthur Burk! Oh, it's Arthur Burk! Get in, Arthur! Get in, Arthur'.*"

You Might Be the Answer to Someone Else's Problem

"*Arthur was happy to get out of the rain but didn't really know what was happening. 'Oh praise God, Arthur,' the people in the car said excitedly. 'We are having a healing meeting in our village, and the man who was coming to preach called from London and said he couldn't make it'.*

"*Arthur still wasn't sure about it all.*

"*Arthur, we were just praying and asking God to send someone to preach at our meeting, because everyone is coming! And, Arthur, suddenly there you were — just standing there in the middle of nowhere. Isn't God so great! He sent us a preacher — you'.*"

God has called us to live in community, so it's no surprise the Holy Spirit will often lead us in a way outside of our focus in order to help someone else in a profound way.

Our problem is that we live in a perpetual state of partial attention, or outright inattention, to the Holy Spirit's leading.

Discussion:

Has the Holy Spirit ever impressed on you to do something that went against all-natural reasoning? Share with the group what happened.

We read about visions of the glory of God in Ezekiel, and it tends to make us think of the acts of the Holy Spirit as being mystical and secretive.

Symbols are used to refer to the Spirit: such as oil, fire, water, or even a dove (John 3: 5-8; Acts 2:1-4; 1 John 2:20). So, it's easy to lose sight of the fact that, far from being merely an influence or representative of the power of God, the Holy Spirit is, in fact, a real person and a full partner in the Trinity.

Fire speaks of His power, and the water speaks of His cleansing. But when referring to His character, He is said to be like a dove, meek and gentle. We are to be wise as serpents but gentle like doves (Matthew 10:16). His Spirit is working in us to form a meek and gentle spirit, which comes from a place of brokenness and humility. With that comes the revelation that without Him, we can do nothing.

The Holy Spirit anointed Jesus for ministry and then allowed Him to be tempted. Receiving a deeper anointing from the Holy Spirit doesn't mean everything will be easy and smooth. In Luke 4:1, after Jesus was baptized and the Spirit descended upon Him, Jesus was led into the wilderness by the Spirit to fast for forty days (the number for trials and testing). After fasting, when He was weak and most vulnerable, Satan came to tempt Him. Jesus was tempted in the same way we are today: body, soul, and spirit. This involves lust of the flesh (body), lust of the eyes (soul), and the pride of life (spirit), which causes a desire for power.

(Hebrews 4:15) After Jesus resisted, scripture says Satan left to wait for a more opportune time. So, Satan is never finished trying to ensnare us. He is always looking for another opportunity. Temptation usually comes when we are most vulnerable or right before God is ready to take us to the next level or promotion.

Dr R. A. Torrey, once dean of Moody Bible Institute, put it this way: *"If the Holy Spirit is a Divine Person and we know it not, we are robbing a Divine Being of the love and adoration which are His due. It is of the highest practical importance whether the Holy Spirit is a power that we, in our ignorance and weakness, are somehow to get hold of and use, or whether the Holy Spirit is a personal Being.... who is to get hold of us and use us. It is of the highest experiential importance.... Many can testify to the blessing that came into their lives when they came to know the Holy Spirit, not merely as a gracious influence...but as an ever-present, loving friend and helper."*

Jesus' life and ministry were dependent on the Holy Spirit.

He was *conceived* by the Holy Spirit (Luke 1: 35); He was *led* by the Spirit (Matthew 4:1); He was *anointed* by the Spirit for service (Acts 10:38); He was *crucified* in the power of the Spirit (Hebrews 9:14); He was *raised* by the power of the Spirit (Romans 1:4, 8:11); He *gave commandments* to His Disciples and Church through the Spirit (Acts 1:2); and He is the one who *poured out* the Holy Spirit on the Church (Acts 2:33). If the Holy Spirit was so important in the life of Christ, how much more important is He in our lives?

One definition of resurrection is "a moral recovery of spiritual truth." God has restored to us through Christ what Adam and Eve lost. Jesus has replaced the lies of the enemy with spiritual truth. We, as Christians, are supernatural beings because of the miracle of new birth. God breathes His life into our spirit, recreating us from the inside out. When we experience the new birth, we open a door and enter a new kingdom.

1 Peter 2:9 (NKJV): *You are a chosen people, a royal priesthood, a holy nation, and God's special possession, that we may declare the praises of Him who called you out of darkness into His wonderful light.* We have experienced spiritual resurrection because we've been called from the kingdom of darkness into the kingdom of light.

We are told to desire the gifts.

The gifts of the Holy Spirit are still available for Christians today and still operating in the church. In fact, 1 Corinthians 14:1 says to *desire* (to burn or pursue ardently) *spiritual gifts, and* 1 Corinthians 13 *says to pursue love.* At salvation, we receive the gift of the Holy Spirit Himself. We must distinguish this gift from the gifts of the Spirit, which are special abilities granted by the Holy Spirit to equip believers for service (1 Corinthians 12:1-31).

1 Corinthians 13 emphasizes ministering in love because people can come across as abrasive when manifesting certain gifts, such as tongues and interpretation of tongues. There is

far more emphasis on the fruit of the Spirit than on the gifts, which equip us for our calling.

Fruit is what the Holy Spirit wants to produce in us because He is more interested in character than in whether or not we prophesy, speak in tongues, or perform other acts of service in the body.

Galatians 5:22

We have to ask for and pursue both gifts and fruit because neither come automatically.

They both come to us only by grace through the working of the Holy Spirit. How do we seek spiritual gifts? We can ask God (1 Corinthians 12:31; 1 Corinthians 14:1,12; James 1:5), or they can be imparted through the laying on of hands (1 Timothy 4:14).

In 1 Corinthians 12:31, we are told to earnestly desire the higher gifts. First, we should *pursue love* so when we do prophesy or have a message in tongues with interpretation, it is done in the right Spirit and not because we want to draw attention to ourselves. All the gifts should operate in harmony with faith, hope, and love.

Discussion:

What are these higher gifts, and are they better than the others?

🫀 **The motivation for asking to receive the gifts of the Holy Spirit should be love.**

It's always a good idea to check your motives and be sure you are not seeking out personal glory. Read Acts 8:19-24 as a cautionary tale about Simon the Sorcerer. We should be pursuing the gifts because we want to be a conduit of blessing. Our motivation should be love for others and wanting what God wants for them. A gift that doesn't operate that way is like a clanging symbol.

In the Tabernacle, the edge of the High Priest's garments had a row of bells alternating with pomegranates to soften the sound. If the bells had been hitting against each other, maybe it would have caused an unpleasant sound. Likewise, when we minister in the gifts, if we are not also exhibiting the fruit of the Spirit, our words will have an irritating instead of soothing effect. This is alluded to in 1 Corinthians 13:1-2.

Prayer: *Lord, help me to have pure motives in ministering to others. Lord, I do earnestly desire the spiritual gifts listed in 1 Corinthians 12 but help me to first be motivated by love. I pray all the gifts the Holy Spirit has for me would manifest in my life and ministry, but most of all that you give me a pure heart in all that I say and do. Show me your heart for those around me, and help me to have a heart-to-heart connection with whomever you put in my path daily. Amen.*

Discussion:

Have you ever questioned your motives in reaching out to others? What would be some reasons we would have motives in ministry that are not pure?

We are told to be filled with the Spirit in Ephesians 5:18-21.

There are two Greek words translated *filled* in the New Testament. One is *pimplemi*, which is used when referring to the Holy Spirit spontaneously coming upon someone for a particular task or purpose (Luke 1:67, Acts 2:4). It represents a temporary empowering. It might be a one-time manifestation of the Spirit in some way, i.e., laughter or dancing.

The other Greek word for *filled* is *pleroo* which means "a frequent, repetitive infilling, a continual inner working of the Spirit within us." It permeates and fills every area of our lives. The disciples were filled in Acts 2:4, and later in Acts 4:31, the same disciples were refilled.

Discussion:

What does it look like to be filled with the Spirit?

We will have supernatural ability in these areas:

1. We will be free to praise Jesus because we will be in love with Him.

2. We will have a thankful heart.

3. Our speech will be different because the Holy Spirit will cause us to guard our words.

4. We will have a heart to serve.

5. We will be hungry for the Word, and it will seem relevant to us.

6. We will no longer struggle to pray.

7. We will want to obey the Father.

8. We will hear His voice more clearly.

9. We will have boldness and confidence.

When these abilities begin to diminish, we become "leaking" vessels. We should ask Jesus to baptize, fill, and refill us with His Spirit. Sometimes the fruit of the Spirit and the power to live in Christlikeness is not evident in our lives because we think what we have already experienced of the Holy Spirit is enough.

The Spirit makes us alive when are born again. It is not enough to receive the Holy Spirit at the new birth; we need to continually be filled with the Holy Spirit. Just like when we drive, if we put fuel in our car just once, we can't expect it to keep going indefinitely. Picture a car running out of gas, sputtering and struggling to keep moving but eventually stopping somewhere along the way because it doesn't have the power to keep going. This is what happens to us spiritually without a constant refilling of the Holy Spirit.

God Moment:

Be still and practice the presence of God.

Beloved, I invite you to sit on My knee and lay your head on My chest. I want to spread My wings over you for warmth, shelter, and protection. There is fresh oil under the shelter of My wings for strength and renewal.

Beloved, don't busy yourself with so many good things that you miss the best thing. There is a time to be busy and a time to be still. I am calling you to be still and hear My heart. Take a moment and listen.

Your strength will be renewed, and you will soar above your circumstances. You will gain a heavenly perspective. You will feel My heart for others.

Ruth 2:12 ; Psalm 36:7; Isaiah 40:31; Luke 10:39-42

Assignment:

1. How have you thought of the Holy Spirit as an impersonal influence in your life?

_____

_____

2. *How does it look to allow the Holy Spirit to control your actions instead of your flesh controlling you?*

_____

_____

3. *What would this feel like?*

_____

_____

4. *What has God used in your life to build character?*

_____

_____

5. *As a result, how did that produce more fruit of the Spirit in your life?*

_____

_____

6. *You received the Holy Spirit at the new birth, but do you feel as if you've **met** the **Person** of the Holy Spirit?*

_____

_____

7. *What does it mean to you to live in the age of the Holy Spirit?*

_____

_____

Final thought:

We need to be continually filled with the Spirit.

Journal:

_____

_____

_____

_____

_____

_____

_____

_____

_____

_____

_____

_____

_____

_____

_____

_____

_____

_____

_____

_____

_____

_____

_____

_____

_____

_____

_____

_____

_____

_____

_____

_____

Lesson 7: Gifts with Purpose

We bless God when we allow the Holy Spirit to bless others through us.

Ways we can grieve the Holy Spirit:

We grieve the Holy Spirit when we willfully sin by falling into serious doctrinal or moral corruption and try to operate in the gifts with wrong motives or while continuing to sin. What comes through will be flawed and inaccurate. If we don't confess our sin and repent, the gifts become corrupt. When repentance comes, the gift will again effectively manifest through us. Sampson is an example. We also grieve the Holy Spirit when we neglect the gift within us (Matthew 25:25-28; 1 Timothy 4:14).

Romans 11:29: *the gifts and calling of God are irrevocable.*

The gifts are given so we can bless others and glorify God.

Prayer: *Lord, please forgive me if I have ever grieved your Spirit in any way. Help me to be obedient to anything I believe You are saying to me. I repent of any sin in my life. Help me not to neglect the gift within me and not be afraid to receive all You have for me. Show me how to use the gifts You've given me to bless others and to serve You by serving them. Amen.*

The indwelling of the Holy Spirit

There are symbols of water associated with the Holy Spirit. When we are born again, the indwelling of the Holy Spirit is described as a well or fountain of water. We see the well of salvation mentioned in Isaiah 12:3. Jesus is at the well in John 4:14 when He tells the Samaritan woman that He will give her water to drink that will become in her a spring of water welling up to eternal life. God's gift to sinners is Jesus, the Savior; His gift to saints is Jesus, the Baptizer. When we are born again, we receive a well of living water within us that should flow out of us to others.

When Jesus baptizes us in the Holy Spirit, the well in us becomes like a river that generates power to be a witness (John 7:37-39). This is when the well of living water flows out of us.

We see the Holy Spirit represented by water in Ezekiel 47:1-12 where he saw in a vision water flowing from the Temple. The "man" led him through the water, ankle deep, knee deep, waist deep, and lastly, it was deep enough to swim in, an impassable river. Wherever the water goes, it brings life. This is an example of us today as temples of the Holy Spirit. 1 Corinthians 3:16: *we are the temple and God's Spirit dwells in u*s. The water represents the Holy Spirit flowing from the throne of God to us (Revelation 22:1). It's up to us how much of the Holy Spirit we want.

The Old Testament picture of how much we want of the Holy Spirit and how deep we want to go is in Ezekiel 47:1-12, when the prophet was brought into the Inner Court, the Holy Place. He could go as deep as he wanted into the water.

How deep do you want to go?

We can apply all of these water levels by letting go of our control and allowing the stream of the Spirit to carry us wherever it wants us to go.

Discussion:

How would these different water levels apply to us after salvation?

1 Corinthians 6:19: *Don't you know that your body is the temple of the Holy Spirit who is in you, whom you have from God, and you are not your own?*

The threshold of the temple represents a door to a new realm of spirituality. A threshold is something we step over to go into a new room or place. When we come to that threshold in our journey with the Lord and move into the next place God has for us, it releases a whole new dimension of the spirit realm in power. This is what happens when we are born again; we go from the natural to the supernatural.

The water flowing from under the threshold of the temple faced east. The gate to the Tabernacle faced east. The east represents Jesus; he sent the Holy Spirit after he ascended. Matthew 24:27: *He will also return from the east.* The water flowed from the right side of the temple. This represents Jesus seated at the right hand of God, pouring out the Spirit on the Day of Pentecost (Acts 2:33).

The water began from under the threshold of the temple toward the east. The east represents Jesus; He sent the Holy Spirit after He was resurrected and went to the Father. We know when the soldiers pierced his side, blood and water flowed out (John 19:34).

However, it's up to us how deep we go into the water of the Holy Spirit. We can accept Christ as Savior and have the Holy Spirit dwelling in us but stay in water that's only ankle, knee, or waist deep. We can control and manage that, or we can go in so deep we have to either swim or go with the flow of the current. You could think of a tub, a swimming pool, a river, or the ocean. Going with the flow means surrendering to the Holy Spirit. The river or the ocean can be a scary thought.

In John 7:38, it says that since we are the temples of the Holy Spirit, out of our heart (some translations say belly) will flow rivers of living water. The water flowing out of the Temple in Ezekiel is a picture of the Holy Spirit flowing from the throne of God to us.

Ezekiel 47:2 tells us the Angel brought Ezekiel out of the north gate and around to the outside to the outer gate that faces east, and there was water running out on the right side. This represents that the Holy Spirit is available to those who are near and far. (Jew and Gentile) The trickle through the power of the Holy Spirit becomes a mighty river with no tributaries flowing into it to add more water. However, the trickle's impact can be weakened by outside influence (a logjam or a dam for instance).

Zechariah 14:8 on that day living water will flow out from Jerusalem, half of it east to the Dead Sea and half of it west to the Mediterranean Sea, in summer and in winter.

Discussion:

How can our impact be affected by outside influence?

The water in Ezekiel 47:3 that came up to his ankles represents salvation. This was a comfortable, easy place to stop and rest. Many in the church today think it is enough to accept Christ as Savior and stay in the ankle-deep water. They have no desire to move deeper into what the Holy Spirit has for them.

God wants us to go deeper, not just test the water.

In Ezekiel 47:4, the Angel brought Ezekiel into deeper water up to his knees. Next, he went in waist-deep. The waist-deep waters represent a position of worship in our innermost being, where we decide if we surrender our will and trust God.

Discussion:

What is God asking you to do that would require a new place of surrender? What would it look like for you to go deeper?

In Ezekiel 47:5, the water became a river he could not cross without swimming because it was too deep. This represents a place of surrendering to the flow of the Spirit, which happens to us when we surrender our lives and allow the Holy Spirit complete control. We trust the Lord to get us where He wants us to go.

Discussion:

Have you ever been here? Was it scary?

(Ezekiel 47:6-7) When he returned to the bank of the river, Ezekiel's spiritual eyes were opened, and he saw trees on both sides of the river. (Normally a desert and barren area.) The Lord wants to open our eyes to see and experience new things in the spirit realm and bring life to some barren areas of our lives.

In Ezekiel 47:8, again water flowed to the eastern region, down into the valley, entering the sea, and when it reached the sea, its waters were healed. We know from Isaiah 61:1-3 that God has called us to bring the good news of gospel salvation and healing to the sea of people around us who are living in the valley of spiritual death. The Holy Spirit will bring life to the dead areas of our souls. Valleys are the places where God brings something beautiful out of our struggles.

(Ezekiel 47:9) Every living thing that moves wherever the river goes will live and be healed. (Literal translations is two rivers) It's possible the river represents salvation and healing (Revelation 22:1-3).

(Ezekiel 47:12) In this imagery, we are the trees God is using to bring a life-giving message of healing and salvation.

This river flowing from the very throne of God represents the source of life. The river came by the altar because that represents the place of sacrifice Jesus made for us. When we really understand that healing and deliverance come from the throne of God, the pressure is off of us. When we trust Him to fill our mouths and use us to meet a need, boldness will come. He is our source of life.

Pastor and author Rachel Burchfield explains it this way: "When Jesus became your Savior, He cleansed your sin by His blood; but when Jesus becomes your Baptizer, He fills you with His Spirit. The result of salvation is forgiveness; the result of the baptism is power."

It's up to us how deeply we want to be immersed in the Holy Spirit; it doesn't affect our salvation. Our choices are:

- *Getting our feet wet* in the Holy Spirit is like salvation, which the well represents (Isaiah 61:1-3).

- *Wading in the water* is like sanctification, which the stream represents (John 17:19; 1 Corinthians 6:11, Hebrews 10:10).

- *Swimming in the water* is like total surrender, which the river represents. The best choice is to let it carry you where He wants you to go (John 4:14, 7:38-39).

He will give us as much as we want (Luke 11:13). We decide.

God will only take you as far as you are willing to go. Ask Him if you are where He wants you to be.

Prayer: *Lord, I repent of my sins and confess my need for a Savior. I ask You to come into my heart and be my well of salvation. Help me to trust You and be willing to be immersed in the river of Your Spirit with total surrender. I want Your living water. Thank you, Amen.*

God Moment

Ask God to reveal things that have been hidden.

Beloved, where the streams of life are rocky, I will pick you up in My arms and carry you so your feet will not be hurt. I will hug you to Myself so you will feel safe. Trust Me to carry you safely.

I want to restore some things from your childhood the enemy stole from you. Those hurts were not My plans for you. I wept when you wept, and I wanted to assure you that I was there.

I will lift you high so you can see what I see in the distance. I'll reveal truth and show you things to come. My thoughts toward you are only for good. Allow Me to speak truth to replace the lies the enemy planted from your past.

Take a moment; ask Me for truth and it will set you free.

John 16: 13-15

Jeremiah 29: 11

Jeremiah 33: 3

Assignment:

1. If you ever feel you are on the threshold of something and haven't quite entered into the new place God is calling you to, the something more, what do you think it might be?

_____

_____

2. If you sense the Lord is calling you to go deeper, and it makes you fearful, why do you think that is?

_____

_____

3. What would going deeper look like for you personally?

_____

_____

4. Journal what He reveals about the lies you have believed about yourself as a result of things that happened in your past. Then journal the truths the Lord reveals to you to replace the lies you believed. Be sure to forgive those who hurt you.

_____

_____

Final thought:

God wants to set us free from our fears and misconceptions.

Journal:

_____

Journal:

Lesson 8: Spiritual Gifts

The gifts of the Holy Spirit manifest in and through believers for the benefit of others who are believers or non-believers.

Spiritual Gifts

I believe, based on Romans 12:3-8 and 1 Corinthians 12:14, that the Holy Spirit gives gifts to every believer for the building up of the body of Christ. These gifts should be exercised according to biblical guidelines and priorities. Also, the Holy Spirit is sovereign and may give any gifts He wants at any time He wants (1 Corinthians 12:11).

The gift of tongues can be used in several ways but is referred to as a single gift. It may be used for cross-cultural evangelism (Acts 2:1-11), private prayer (1 Corinthians 14:3, 14-19, 28), or for ministry to the body when an interpreter is present (1 Corinthians 14:5). Not everyone must speak in tongues (1 Corinthians 12:30).

The gift of tongues is probably the most controversial gift of the Holy Spirit.

The Greek word Paul uses in Corinthians that is most often translated as "tongues" literally means "languages." It means to speak in a language not known to you otherwise. Speaking in tongues is not an out-of-control, ecstatic utterance that causes a person to lose control. It is a form of communication that bypasses the mind and comes from your spirit. The sound may change depending on what you are praying about.

My goal is to help us better understand this gift. I'd encourage you to examine the scriptures and decide for yourself what you believe about the gift of tongues, which is also referred to as receiving a personal prayer language. Personal prayer language is you speaking to God and, therefore, doesn't need an interpretation since God has no problem understanding what you are saying. Having a personal prayer language does not necessarily mean your new language will ever be used as the gift of tongues for the assembly. That would need an interpretation because otherwise, how would the congregation know what God is saying to them (1 Corinthians 14:2-18)?

There are several views on what John the Baptist says about the Baptism of the Holy Spirit in the New Testament and what this means for us as believers. When asking to be baptized in the Holy Spirit, the evidence you received what you asked for will usually be a personal prayer language, but not always. You may experience that later. However, you will definitely receive more of the Holy Spirit. See Matthew 3:11; Mark 1:8; Luke 3:16; and John 1:33.

Some churches accept all of the gifts in 1 Corinthians 12 as being valid for today, except the gift of tongues.

Scripture says in 1 Corinthians 12:13 that the Holy Spirit baptizes you into the Body of Christ, and it says there is only one baptism into the Body of Christ by the Holy Spirit. This is referring to salvation; we can only be born again once, and we receive the Holy Spirit at that time.

In the early centuries of the church, people frequently had a new language accompany their salvation experience. Usually, when they were water baptized, they came up out of the water speaking in a new language. We rarely have that happen today, probably because of our Western worldview, but I believe it's still available to us. We just don't realize it or expect it.

We see in Acts 19 where Paul found some disciples in Ephesus and asked if they had received the Holy Spirit since they believed. They said, "No, we have not even heard that there is a Holy Spirit." He asked into what baptism they had been baptized, and they answered, "John's baptism." Paul told them that John baptized with the baptism of repentance, telling the people to believe in the one who was to come after him, Jesus. Then, after they were baptized in the name of the Lord Jesus, he laid hands on them, and they began to speak in tongues and even prophesied. We are told there were about twelve of them. This is proof that everyone does not receive the Baptism of the Holy Spirit at the same time they are born again.

In Matthew 3:11 it says it's Jesus who baptizes you with the Holy Spirit. This baptism can happen at salvation when the Holy Spirit baptizes you into the body of Christ, or it can happen at a later time.

In the Western church community, this seems to happen when we are ready to go deeper in the Spirit and are seeking more of the Holy Spirit's power in our lives. Both baptisms require a step of faith into the spirit realm. One when we accept Christ as Savior and the other when we move deeper into what He has for us.

Jesus baptizes us into the Holy Spirit; the Holy Spirit baptizes us into the Body of Christ.

Discussion:

If you believe there is more to experience of the Holy Spirit, what would that look like in your personal life? Share with the group, or, if it's too personal, journal about it later.

Jack Hayford says in his book, *The Beauty of Spiritual Language,* "It is a distinct ministry of the Holy Spirit to flow into the inner recesses of our beings and to bring to the surface anything that would obstruct our growth in grace and remove it. He wants to help bring to the surface everything that would advance the Father's purpose in us but which has been buried by the turbulence or contrary streams of our past experiences or ignorance."

Sometimes we have logjams in our heart that only the Holy Spirit can remove.

Let's look more at tongues as a personal spiritual language.

This is something the Bible teaches, but many of us struggle with understanding it. These two scriptures describe the benefits: self-edification (1 Corinthians 14:4) and building one's personal faith (Jude 20).

Praying to God in your spiritual language has been compared to a power-producing plant within us that generates the power of God like the Hoover Dam pumps electricity.

Interestingly, the fastest-growing denominational branch of the church in the world is Pentecostal. People groups in the rest of the world understand the spirit realm better than our Western culture, and, as a result, they are more open. They've seen the realm of darkness and know they need all the power and resources from the Lord that He's made available to us as believers.

In Acts, there are five accounts describing the receiving of the Holy Spirit.

Four of the five accounts indicate those receiving the Holy Spirit spoke in tongues:

- Acts 2:4, the upper room.

- Acts 8:14, the Samaritans.

- Acts 9:17-20, Paul after Ananias prayed for him (It doesn't actually say Paul spoke in tongues at that time, but we know he did at some point because he said in 1 Corinthians 14:18 that he thanked God that he prayed in tongues more than everyone.)

- Acts 10:44-48, the Gentiles.

- Acts 19:1-7, Disciples in Ephesus.

Distinguishing between personal prayer language versus the gift of tongues with interpretation

As stated earlier, scripture isn't clear on this, but there seems to be a difference in the devotional tongues we receive when we ask Jesus to baptize us in the Holy Spirit and the Gift of Tongues described in 1 Corinthians 12 that's to be used in an assembly (Mark 16:17; Acts 2:4; Acts 10:44-46; Acts 19:6; 1 Corinthians 14:2, 4).

When praying in a personal prayer language, *we* are speaking *to* God. The gift of tongues, when used in the assembly, is when *God* is speaking *through* us to the group, therefore needing an interpretation to be effective.

After all, if there is no interpretation of what is being said, who would benefit? So, when the Bible says that Jesus will baptize believers in the Holy Spirit, with the evidence being speaking in tongues, it seems to mean that He is imparting a personal prayer language. However, having a personal prayer language does not necessarily mean one would ever use the gift of tongues in the assembly.

Most who have a spiritual language will use this gift to speak to God during private prayer time only (1 Corinthians 14: 2, 12, 25, 39).

Prophecy, unlike tongues, is spoken in a language known to the one speaking and to whoever is the recipient.

When the gift of tongues is used in the assembly, there needs to be an interpretation. "Yet in the church" is a key phrase indicating that tongues were spoken without an interpretation in places other than the church service.

However, in church, prophecy (a message from the Lord that has been communicated to a person or group by the Holy Spirit) is more beneficial because no one has to interpret. Again, when tongues are spoken in the church to a group of people, there needs to be an interpretation of what was said.

1 Corinthians 14:14: *For if I speak in another language, my spirit prays, but my mind is unfruitful.*

When our spirit prays, it isn't filtered through our mind because our personal prayer language comes up out of our spirit. We are communicating with God from spirit to Spirit.

A message in tongues for the congregation comes from the Holy Spirit through us to (and for) the assembly and needs an interpretation so they will know what the Lord is saying. This also doesn't originate in our mind, but it rises up out of our spirit inspired by the Holy Spirit.

If the gift of tongues and our prayer language were the same gifts, why would God give us something we would never have the opportunity to use? Most people who have a personal prayer language will never have a message in tongues for a group of people needing an interpretation.

Sometimes personal prayer language can also be used in corporate praise. You might hear personal prayer languages during a worship service where people are more open to expressing praise in that way. The gift of tongues in 1 Corinthians 12:10 are called divers (diversities, or different kinds) of tongues. They include recognizable languages as well as those not recognizable. Individual tongues for the believer may change over time. Usually, when someone first receives a prayer language, it doesn't sound much like a language. In time, it will develop into sounding more like one. However, it won't be a language already known to the person speaking it.

Discussion:

If you have ever heard someone speak in tongues, how were you affected by the experience?

We have seen two extremes with this gift: some believers ignore it by deciding it is not for today, or conversely, some put too much emphasis on the gift.

There are many misconceptions and fears about receiving a prayer language.

- Some believe this gift is not for them personally, so they don't expect to receive.

- Some are seeking the gift and not the Giver.

- Some think they have to be more spiritual to receive.

- Some think they are not good enough to receive.

- Some think they have to wait and earn it.

- Some think it's not for today.

- Some fear receiving a counterfeit.

- Some reject their experience because they don't think it was real.

- Some are deceived into believing nothing happened.

To be clear, the gift of tongues with interpretation has a different purpose from the gift of tongues for your personal prayer language.

Tongues with interpretation is the Utterance/Ministry Gift in 1 Corinthians 12 and 1 Corinthians 14. It is one of three vocal gifts and involves speaking out in an assembly with a message for someone or the entire group.

Again, it should always have an interpretation; otherwise, if no one understands what is being said, there is no benefit. (Read 1 Corinthians 14:12-14, 18-19) Paul says in verses 18 and 19 that he speaks in tongues *more than you all, yet in the church* he would rather speak so others could understand what he was saying.

The gift of tongues with interpretation is spoken in a language not known to the one speaking. It may or may not be recognized as a known language to those listening. The interpretation usually comes through someone else. However, in some cases, the same person giving the message in tongues also interprets the message. Interpretation of the message is not an exact translation or transliteration.

The gift of tongues with interpretation is referred to as the lesser gift because when a person prophesies, you don't need an interpretation. Therefore, when spoken together, tongues and interpretation are essentially the same as one person doing prophecy. Like prophecy, it edifies and builds up the church (1 Corinthians 14:5). The one giving the message may also pray to interpret it (1 Corinthians 14:13).

 The main thing is to get plugged into the Power Source — whatever that looks like for you and however God wants to do it.

God Moment

Allow the Lord to help you relax so you can receive whatever He wants to do.

Come into My Courtyard and dance with Me. Put your head on My shoulder and place your feet on Mine. Allow Me to lead. Can you hear the music? It's a symphony of My thoughts about you and how I sing over you.

I want to give you a drink from My fountain. There is a pool here for healing. Take a moment and step in. Let My healing presence flow from your feet up to the top of your head.

Can you smell the flowers I'm putting in your hair? I'm holding a bouquet over your head and crushing the flowers so the nectar will fall down over you. It's My fragrance all over you. When you leave My presence, it will go with you so others will know you have been with Me.

Song of Solomon 4:11

Assignment:

1. List the things you have been taught personally about the gift of tongues.

_____

_____

2. If you sense the Lord is calling you to go deeper and it makes you fearful, why do you think that is?

_____

_____

3. List the questions you have about the use of tongues as a personal prayer language.

_____

_____

4. Have you asked for this gift and felt that you didn't receive anything, or what came out of your mouth didn't sound like a language? Explain.

_____

_____

5. List some reservations you might have about it.

_____

_____

Final thought:

God wants you to have all He has for you; this means what He has done for others, He will do for you.

Acts 10:34

Journal:

_____

_____

_____

_____

_____

_____

_____

_____

_____

_____

_____

_____

_____

_____

_____

_____

_____

_____

_____

_____

_____

_____

_____

_____

_____

_____

_____

_____

_____

_____

_____

_____

_____

Journal:

_____

_____

_____

_____

_____

_____

_____

_____

_____

_____

_____

_____

_____

_____

_____

_____

_____

_____

_____

_____

_____

_____

_____

_____

_____

_____

_____

_____

_____

_____

_____

_____

Lesson 9: Baptisms

We've looked at water representing or personified as the Holy Spirit. Now let's look at the Holy Spirit symbolized by fire. In Matthew 3:11, John says, *I baptize you with water for repentance. But after me will come one who is more powerful than I, whose sandals I am not fit to carry. He will baptize you with the Holy Spirit and with fire.*

What is this baptism of fire? *His winnowing fork is in his hand, and he will clear his threshing floor, gathering his wheat into the barn and burning up the chaff with unquenchable fire.*

In Isaiah 4:4 it says the Lord will wash away the filth of the women of Zion; He will cleanse the bloodstains from Jerusalem by a spirit of judgment and a spirit of fire.

A picture in nature of what God does in us supernaturally is a forest fire. In God's overall design for the ecosystem, He uses fire as a major disturbance to initiate new beginnings.

Ron Hay, the University of Tennessee Professor Emeritus of Forestry, explained actual forest fires this way:

"A forest fire creates conditions for the new. There is what are called 'prescribed fires' to accomplish goals for purging and new growth that hopefully don't get out of control. A fire purges the bad seed to create the new. The new isn't always the same species as the old. There might be a new grouping of plants and trees, even flowers. Many times, it will look nothing like what was burned up. It might be generations before the old shows up again.

"There are some species that can only grow from ashes. There are some pines that will disappear out of the eco system unless a fire happens at some point in time (might be ten plus years). Fire is the biggest major natural disturbance there is."

Similarly, the Lord will use the Holy Spirit to search, illuminate, refine, and consume the dross, or waste, in our character and lives when He takes possession of us. We experience a baptism of fire, causing us to die to ourselves and make room for the new.

Then, we can allow the Lord to do whatever it takes to make us more like Him. What God brings up from the ashes of our old ways and thinking will look different. With the new growth will come a new perspective. However, the new growth may not appear as quickly as we would like.

In Hebrews 6:2, in the New King James Version, it refers to a doctrine of baptisms (plural). There is a water baptism and a spirit baptism. John's baptism of water was about salvation, coming up out of the water as a new creation, leaving the old life behind, and rising up to new life. John's baptism of water was an outward sign, while Jesus' baptism was internal. John immerses his followers in water, while Jesus immerses His followers in the Holy Spirit. In Luke 3:15-18, John the Baptist refers to the Baptism of the Holy Spirit as the Baptism by Jesus.

We are also told that He will baptize us with the Holy Spirit and fire (Matthew 3:11). I believe being baptized by fire is a refining process God allows to make us more like Him.

In 1 Corinthians 12:13, we read about being baptized into one Body, the Body of Christ, which is the Church and is an act of the Holy Spirit when you become a believer. In Mark 10:38, Jesus refers to a baptism of suffering, which refers to persecution for His name's sake, and perhaps for some, this is the baptism of fire.

My testimony: Deuteronomy 6:5 says, "You shall love the Lord your God with all your heart, with all your soul, and with all your strength." I knew I didn't love the Lord with all my heart, soul, and strength, so after confessing this to the Lord, I asked Him to help me love Him that way. As a result, when I met the person of the Holy Spirit, He made me fall more in love with Jesus. Some major changes happened in me. The Bible came alive and current, my prayer life changed, my heart was in tune with His, and I had more desire to be obedient to His Word. God changed my behavior in ways that empowered me to be a witness and influence others. I considered my words before saying hurtful or spiteful things. I began to change how I dressed because my clothes didn't honor Him. I cleaned up my language, which definitely did not glorify the Lord. My husband also began to notice my improved attitude. I had less anger and more joy and peace. I also no longer had to get the last word in. When each person has their own encounter with the Holy Spirit, it will be what they need to be closer to the Lord and glorify Him.

The following account is my own personal experience: *My initial prayer language was an Aztec phrase, but I didn't know that at the time. I just kept praying it over and over, believing by faith I had received a new language even though it didn't sound like anything I had ever heard. After searching for many years for the meaning of what language I was speaking, I was in Mexico City on a mission trip when I heard one of the youth pastors use the same phrase while preaching. Afterward, I ran up to him to ask him what the phrase meant. He said it was Aztec and meant "mighty warrior of God." At the time, I had no idea why God would have me saying that phrase over and over again in prayer. Now, years later, I think He wanted me to become a prayer warrior. I believe He was having me pray that way so my faith would be built up (Jude 20) to pray for people to receive healing and be set free from strongholds in their lives.*

Since the mid-seventies, I have been privileged to pray for others to be set free from inner hurts and the resulting lies from the enemy, which formed strongholds in their lives. God had supernaturally imparted the faith I needed to believe the enemy could be defeated in their lives through prayer.

*It could be that the "Baptism of the Holy Spirit" does **in us** and **for us** what God wants to accomplish in and through us. I believe that was true for me. Some refer to these breakthrough experiences with the Holy Spirit as the "Baptism of the Holy Spirit," while others may not use this term. What matters is the degree of personal relationship one has with Christ. If you permit Him, God will take you on whatever path is necessary for you to get there.*

Genesis 2:7: *And the LORD God formed man of the dust of the ground, and breathed into his nostrils the breath of life.*

When we ask the Lord to baptize us in the Holy Spirit, it's a one-time request, but being filled with the Spirit is a constant. When you ask, you receive whether you speak in a prayer language or not (Acts 10:34). You still get what you ask for from the Lord because He is no respecter of persons, that is, God isn't partial. Also, you may receive a personal prayer language without ever asking Jesus to baptize you with the Holy Spirit. We can't put God in a box; He can do whatever, whenever He wants. Either way, you will become more empowered by the Holy Spirit.

The following scriptures refer to the Holy Spirit:

The old creation began with the breath of God (Genesis 2:7), and in John 1:33, the new creation began with the breath of God the Son. The *Old Covenant related externally*; the law was written on stone, and the Spirit would come on people and then depart. The *New Covenant relates internally*; the law is written on our hearts, and the Spirit enters into us and remains.

We have a new life through the indwelling Holy Spirit.

Jesus enters into our lives as the Holy Spirit once we place our faith in Him (Ephesians 1:13). He then gives us spiritual gifts that enable us to serve others (1 Corinthians 12:4-6).

The gift of tongues may be received at salvation like in Acts 10:44-46 with Cornelius' household, who were the first Gentiles to accept Christ, then spoke in tongues.

Or, the gift of tongues may be received later, after salvation, as the believers did in Samaria after Philip preached, as in Acts 8:5-8. We see it happen again in Ephesus around 54 A.D. when Paul preached to some disciples there (Acts 19:1-3, 6).

The gift of tongues is the only one of the 1 Corinthians 12 gifts not in operation in the Old Testament unless we see a picture of this new language at the Tower of Babel. In Genesis 11:1-3 all of humanity spoke one language common to all. Some believe it was Hebrew, because of the similarity to the Semitic Akkadian language, which is related to the Semitic languages of Hebrew and Arabic, according to jewishlink.news.

The people were in complete unity under the leadership of Nimrod. Because the people had one language common to all, it became a vehicle Satan used through Nimrod to unite them in rebellion against the Word of God. Having the same language gave his followers power.

In Genesis 11:4, we see the people of Babylon in agreement to build a city. (Babylon was an influential city located near the Euphrates River, sixty miles south of Bagdad in what is now Iraq. It served as a center of Mesopotamian civilization for two millennia). The intent was to make a name for them and prevent being scattered abroad over the face of the earth. This was in direct rebellion to, and the opposite of, what God had said to Adam and Noah. In Genesis 1:22 and again in Genesis 9:1, 7, mankind was told to be fruitful and multiply to populate the earth — i.e., move out from the cities. Nimrod wanted to establish a center of worship (of himself) meant to keep the people in one place.

Nimrod is a picture of Satan using a man to try to exalt his own throne above God's heavenly one (Isaiah 14:13).

Satan tried to get Jesus to buy into the lie that he could make Jesus God over this earthly realm when he tempted Him in the wilderness. Satan offered Jesus an earthly kingdom and power. At Jesus' baptism God said, *this is my beloved Son*. However, Satan tried to question his identity by saying *if* you are the Son of God. But Jesus knew He was already God, and that He would have an earthly kingdom given to him by His Father. He didn't need Satan to give him kingdoms and power.

Like Nimrod, the religious leaders of Jesus' day had exalted themselves over the people to rule and bring judgment. In Micah 4:2-5 we see that Jesus will bring peace, the opposite of the enemy using Nimrod to bring war to humanity.

God came down and confused their speech.

Confusing their language at the Tower of Babel was a supernatural event by God to divide the people. The Babylonian's thoughts were the same, but they couldn't communicate with each other except with those having the same tongue. Babel means "mixed up or confused." The word used for confound means "mingle or mix." Surely the mixture of new languages sounded confusing to those who spoke a different language. It also must have felt very weird to those speaking in a new tongue/language. As a result, the people were forced to scatter; God intended to separate them physically so they would not be unified in worshipping a false god and building an unholy kingdom. Satan wanted to use Nimrod to establish his kingdom on the earth through man, but God thwarted his plan.

God accomplished his purposes by giving new tongues/languages to the people. It was a good thing because it caused people to disperse, which is what God originally intended for mankind. Perhaps that brought a different kind of unity. It definitely stopped Satan's plans for mankind.

On the Day of Pentecost, the Holy Spirit came down upon the believers in the upper room and gave them a gift of spiritual language meant to reverse the curse on man and bring unity by crossing the barriers of speech.

When the disciples spoke to the multitudes, the people heard them speaking in their own language. Again, there was a supernatural event of tongues. However, unlike the tower of Babel, this one was meant to be a vehicle to bring surrender to the Word of God and gather the people back to Him, not to separate them from each other. It was to bring spiritual unity among believers. Tongues are meant to be a vehicle to bring us closer to God and empower us to be a witness.

One thing is certain. The enemy is afraid of this particular gift and has used it to cause division, the opposite of what God intended. In Acts 2:6-11 we see that spiritual language can sound confusing and weird to those hearing and to those experiencing it for the first time. This is because we are learning a new language. This gift is meant to glorify God; instead, the enemy has used it to bring separation in the Body of Christ. Zephaniah 3:9: *then I will purify the lips of the peoples, that all of them may call on the name of the Lord and serve Him shoulder to shoulder.*

Discussion:

How does God use the gift of tongues to bring unity? How has it sometimes brought division instead?

Some have used 1 Corinthians 13 to validate not believing the gifts are for today. But in doing so, I believe we miss the point of these verses. They were given to do just the opposite and encourage the use of these gifts. But the admonition is to be motivated by love when exercising them. It is not meant to say we no longer have or need them.

One of our biggest challenges as humans is clear communication.

The enemy will take our words and try to cause the other person to hear something different than we said. He will use the gift of tongues against God and us by causing misunderstanding and offense. Some teach that tongues are clear communication from our spirit to God or from God to men. Whatever God intended, it requires a total surrender through an act of faith.

So, to be clear, having a spiritual language does not make one super-spiritual. It does not mean that one who does not practice a spiritual language is less spiritual than one who does. We are not saying that believers have to speak in tongues.

Purpose of a personal spiritual language (tongues)

A personal prayer language can be used in private devotion, especially when we don't know what to pray (1 Corinthians 14:1-3, 18, 19). It will assist us in worshipping and praising God. It does not require an interpretation, but we may ask the Lord for one so we can understand (1 Corinthians 14:13-15, 27-28, 40). It gives us power to be a witness (Acts 1:8). The gift of the Holy Spirit is for God's *power* see Luke 24:49 and Mark 16:16-18. The fruit of the Spirit is for *holiness*, which all believers should exhibit.

Some are so wary of the New Age movement that they resist having or using a spiritual language, but when we ask for this gift, we don't have to fear receiving a counterfeit (Luke 11:9-13). When we ask God for something, He gives us what we ask for because it is a gift. We don't have to earn it because He wants us to be equipped to minister to others.

Another reason this gift is important is that it builds faith (Jude 20).

In the Old Testament Tabernacle in the wilderness, the High Priest wore special garments that included a robe. The hem of the robe had a pomegranate and a bell around the edge of it. The sound of it could be heard when Aaron, the first High Priest, went into the Most Holy Place.

The Most Holy Place, where the Ark of the God was kept, was, for the early Jews, the literal presence of God as He lived among His people. Only once a year was anyone allowed in, and if he made a mistake, according to the rules given by God, he would be instantly killed.

The fruit between the bells on the robe softened the sound as he moved about. (The High Priest's garment is described in Exodus 28.) Rabbinic tradition says that if the other priests didn't hear the sound of the bells, they pulled him out by a string attached to his ankle because if the other priests went into the Most Holy Place, they would die.

I believe the bells represent the gifts of the Spirit, and the pomegranates represent the fruit of the Spirit. Pomegranates were also seen in the Temple Solomon built as part of the decorations. Today, when we move out as priests on behalf of others and minister in the gifts of the Spirit, if our motivation is love, we bring a pleasant sound. If it is for any other reason, it sounds more like a clanging symbol. Love should be our motivation for desiring spiritual gifts.

Both the gifts and the fruit of the Spirit should be evident in every believer's life.

The veil separating Aaron's sons from the Most Holy Place was torn in two from top to bottom when Jesus died on the cross (Matthew 27:51). Hebrews says that because the veil has been torn, we can go into the presence of the Lord any time we want (Hebrews 6:19-20).

Our hearts — His gifts

The bells and pomegranates on the High Priest's garment indicate that spiritual gifts need to be exhibited from a heart of compassion and love for those on the receiving end of the gifts.

When you pray in your prayer language, your mind is not forming the words coming out of your mouth. They originate in your spirit. However, your mind might be praying in English at the same time. We can all say that we don't always pray with our minds in a way that produces fruit. Sometimes our prayers are self-centered and fleshly — more about what we want. We can also remedy that by asking the Holy Spirit to pray through us in our native tongue as well as our prayer language.

Receiving the gift of tongues will not make you super-spiritual, but it will mean that you can now pray in the natural and in the supernatural. Exhibiting the fruit of the Spirit is a sign of being spiritually mature. I know people who do not practice this gift and who are much more mature and spiritual than people who do.

If the idea of a personal prayer language is new to you, ask the Lord about it. Ask if this is something he wants you to have. If you went through these steps and felt nothing happened, ask your group leader to pray with you about it (Romans 2:11). It does not mean you do not deserve it or that God doesn't want you to have it. The important thing is not to feel you are somehow lacking. It's just one more tool in your belt that I believe is available to you.

Prayer: *Lord Jesus, I thank you for saving me, and I repent and renounce any occult involvement in my life, no matter how seemingly innocent it might have been or how young I was. I ask you to baptize me in the Holy Spirit with the evidence of a spiritual prayer language. I want all you have for me. I thank you that when I ask for bread, you won't give me a stone, so I thank you that I will not experience a counterfeit* (Matthew 7:9). *Amen.*

Now picture Jesus, then open your mouth and begin to praise Him.

Author's note: This content represents my personal beliefs and experiences. They are not intended to challenge or refute others' convictions on the topic. One of the gifts of Christian fellowship is to be able to live with a diversity of viewpoints on non-essential issues while being fully committed to Christ and one another. Please prayerfully seek the Lord to determine your own convictions related to private prayer language and its universal availability to believers.

God Moment

Ask the Lord for confidence that the blood of Jesus is your protection.

My blood is like a force field. It's a shield around you protecting you from the enemy. When you activate it, he can't get past the shield. If you don't even know it's there, you won't know to activate it. Take a moment and ask.

Faith forms a shield to repulse Satan's attacks. My power is released against your spiritual enemies in the heavens through your obedience and faith in me.

Grace is the force that releases the shield. My blood has cleansed your conscience so you can come into My presence expecting to be received. You have confidence that I am on your side. You know you can't defeat the enemy because you are not strong enough to overcome him; you win because My strength is made perfect in your weakness.

While you stand on my Word, I will fight for you.

2 Corinthians 12:9

1 John 1:7

Ephesians 2: 19; 6: 16

Assignment:

1. *What do you find confusing about the gift of tongues as a personal prayer language?*

   _____

   _____

2. *Are you afraid to ask for this gift? Why or why not?*

   _____

   _____

3. *Why do you think the enemy wants to cause so much strife and division over this particular gift?*

   _____

   _____

Final thought:

I personally believe that the manifestation of a personal prayer language is available for anyone who desires it, though not everyone will speak for God to a group of people (tongues with an interpretation). It is mostly for private use to edify and build us up.

1 Corinthians 12:30, 14:5, 18;

Jude 1:20

Journal:

Section Three

Topic Three: Living a Life of Faith

The gift of faith is like a mustard seed that must be planted, watered, fertilized, protected, and pruned.

Lesson 10: God Responds to Our Faith

In Indiana Jones*: The Last Crusade,* there is a scene where we see Harrison Ford looking into a deep cavern. He needs to get to the other side, but there doesn't seem to be a way. He goes ahead and takes that first step to cross over, and as he does, a bridge appears under his feet, which enables him to get across.

Faith is taking that first step without seeing what is ahead.

Hebrews 11:1: *now faith is confidence in what we hope for and assurance about what we do not see.* Faith flows out of grace. Belief and faith are not the same. Belief opens the door to grace, which in turn, enables faith. Faith is like taking that first step without seeing what is ahead. Grace is the bridge; it is God's response to our faith. In the film, *The Last Crusade,* Ford's part was to act by taking that first step. Otherwise, he would never have seen the bridge that was already there. This is very much what it is like to walk with God and trust Him. God goes ahead of us and supplies everything we need. The bridge materialized after he took that first step and extended his foot to step down. That is how faith works. It is a gift from the Holy Spirit. What happens as a result is supernatural.

"Grace is opposed to earning; it is not opposed to effort." (Dallas Willard)

True spiritual faith flows out of the spirit and affects the mind.

Many people pray for more faith, but we already have all the faith we need. His faith lives in my spirit as an incorruptible

119

seed (1 Peter 1:23). Jesus lives in me, and He has all the faith I need. Hebrews 12:2: *look to Him because He is the author and finisher of my faith.* He holds me up when I am weak because He is faithful to me. In Romans 3:28, it says *the just shall live by faith.* We are justified because of the cross, the sign of His faithfulness. My faith is not in my faith or efforts but in Him and His love for me. New Covenant grace is God's faith in man because He has given us power to be a witness.

Romans 4:16 says *it (God's promise) is of faith that it might be according to grace,* which means that faith occurs when we cease trying to do something by our own efforts and trust Him to do it for us. It is the one attitude that is the opposite of trusting ourselves. It is an attitude of the heart flowing from grace — an entirely free gift of God. The bridge that appeared in the movie was already there, but he couldn't see it until he gave up control of his destiny and moved forward in blind faith.

It's hard to believe in what we can't see.

Trusting in our own effort can result in legalism, the efforts that are meant to control our circumstances or manipulate God Himself. Legalism in religion is living from the outside in. Grace through redemption enables us to live supernaturally from the inside out.

We live in the age of grace and not under the legalism that man attached, then overflowed to the law.

Discussion:

If you were brought up in a legalistic home, how has that influenced how you live as a Christian?

It takes faith to please God (Hebrews 11:6). We first have to believe that He exists and that He will reward us if we seek

Him. We must also believe He cares about us in every detail of our lives. It takes faith to accept grace. Faith is the conduit for grace to flow into us and overflow out of us to others.

Faith is a gift of His grace.

We are saved by God's grace through faith. Faith is in the soil of the heart that receives the gift of God, and God, through His Spirit, prepares the soil to receive the gift. Everything begins and ends with God. All we need to do is cooperate. Jesus was the promised seed that would crush Satan, but He had to die first and be planted in the ground. When things looked hopeless, that seed was resurrected; He was raised from the dead into newness of life. The seed of faith comes from Him (John 3:16). If I know I have the seed of faith in me, then I know whatever I need is in that seed. Hebrews 12:2 says *Jesus is the author and finisher of our faith.*

Faith works through love. Where does that kind of love come from? It comes from the Holy Spirit because Romans 5:5 says that *the love of God has been poured out within our hearts through the Holy Spirit, which was given to us.* Scripture tells us that *every good and perfect gift is from above* James 1:17. Grace is one of those perfect gifts.

True faith is to have faith in God's faithfulness.

When we pray for people's healing, and they are healed, it is not because we had great faith, it is because of grace. The faith we need is to believe that it is up to God, and our part is to obey and have faith in His ability. It's up to Him to bring results, not us.[1]

---

1 For more background on healing and deliverance throughout Church history, see Appendix.

We can operate in a counterfeit faith or a true faith. We can have faith that our religious rules and legalism will work for us, or we can have faith in God's faithfulness. One results in pride, and the other results in humility and love. Faith that trusts in God's ability, coming from either the one receiving or the one conducting healing prayer, gets it done for the one receiving and the one asking God to do it for them.

For instance, we don't have to wonder if our faith or their faith is enough to get a person healed because it all comes back to Him.

Acts 4:33 says that *great grace and great power were received after being filled with the Holy Spirit.* Luke 2:40 and Acts 11:23 refer to the power of God as a result of grace. Great power comes from great grace and results in miracles. We are saved by grace and grace is manifested in a greater dynamic way where the Holy Spirit is at work in power. Sometimes we are just spectators.

Zechariah 4:6-7: *this is the word of the Lord to Zerubbabel; not by might nor by power, but by my Spirit, says the Lord Almighty. What are you, mighty mountain? Before Zerubbabel you will become level ground. Then he will bring out the capstone to shouts of 'God bless it! God bless it!*

Now we need only to speak to obstacles we face as an act of faith. We speak the Word, and the results are His.

For example, in Exodus 17:6, in the wilderness, when the Israelites complained about not having water, God told Moses He would stand on the rock. Then, He commanded Moses to *strike* the rock so water would come forth out of it. However, the second time the Israelites needed water, God told Moses *to speak* to the rock, not strike it (Numbers 20:8). The spoken word was to be the vehicle of the miracle. Striking it brought results, but God was displeased with Moses' disobedience. The Rock represented Jesus (1 Corinthians 10:1-4).

Moses striking it the second time they needed water instead of speaking to it was a sign of unbelief and disrespect. In his frustration and anger, Moses forgot it had nothing to do with him other than obedience to God's spoken Word. When God says to do something in a different way, we must obey because he always has a reason. We are living epistles called to be examples to others. Moses' obedience was to be a picture of "faith in action" of God's grace being poured (1 Peter 5:3).

Striking the rock a second time was a serious offense of disobedience because the rock represented Jesus being crucified for us and pouring out the Holy Spirit on the Church. He cannot be crucified for us again, therefore, now we speak and ask for what we need, which is what Moses was told to do (Hebrews 6:4-6).

God himself stood on the rock as Moses struck it. As a result, the water that poured out was a picture of Jesus sending the Holy Spirit on the Day of Pentecost after he had been struck and bruised for us. In 1 Corinthians 10:4, it says *they all drank the same spiritual drink; for they drank of a spiritual rock that followed them: and the rock was Christ.* Now, all we need to do is pray and thank Him for the outpouring of the Spirit.

Discussion:

How do you think this scripture impacts us today?

Faith like a mustard seed involves cultivating.

Cultivating includes planting, watering, fertilizing, and pruning. The work of the Trinity is involved, but we also have a part. Our part is not resisting the work of the Holy Spirit but using the faith we already have been given.

"A farmer will never leave a field untended after the harvest and expect a new healthy crop to grow the following year. It must be cleared, ploughed up, made ready with any necessary fertilizer, and sown with new seed. So with us, as we yield ourselves to our 'Master Gardener' and allow the Lord to do His work in us we can expect our lives to bear eternal fruit. Our Father transforms us from the inside out as we "let go" of our selfish desires and predilections. When we yield in peaceful surrender and allow His life to soak right through us by His Spirit, we find that His light and wisdom and truth begin to illumine our days and to brighten our world. A new and beautiful crop of righteousness grows in our life, for His glory." (Wayne Evans)

A common farming method at that time was to sow the seed without first plowing the ground. So, the seed fell on various kinds of ground that wasn't prepared to receive the seed.

Read Mark 4:3-8.

Cultivating: Allowing the Holy Spirit to plow the soil of our heart and prepare it for growth.

It says in Revelation that the Bride makes herself ready, so, as the Bride, we have a responsibility to yield to making ourselves ready. We have to be willing to receive the seed and allow the soil to yield a crop. We give the Spirit permission to burn out the old seed by first plowing up wrong thinking, like forest rangers setting a prescribed fire. He draws us to God, and

He plows up the field to reveal our inner man. It's an ongoing process with us, weeding out sin, attitudes, wrong thinking, and being accountable.

Psalms 37:3: *trust in the Lord and do well; dwell in the land and cultivate His faithfulness.*

Feed on His faithfulness, and His truth will produce a harvest. When you do, your garden will look different; there will be no weeds.

There may be a wilderness between what God has promised and living in the fulfillment of that promise. Things may appear to get worse before they get better. It may seem the opposite is happening. This is a good time to develop the fruit of patience and self-control.

God Moment

Ask for faith to trust God totally.

I ride on the wings of eagles. Come, sit up here with Me, and let Me give you a new perspective. Feel the wind of My Spirit taking you where I want you to go. Take a moment and experience the joy and elation of trusting Me.

See, things are not what you thought they were. I'm working them for your good because I love you. Keep your heart and mind open. Do not be afraid of what the future holds; I have you in a safe place. Go with the flow. Let us soar together in the heavens.

Take a moment and enjoy the view.

Exodus 19:4; Psalms 18:10

Assignment:

1. *Why is it hard to grasp that faith flows from grace?*

_____

_____

2. *What would keep you from praying for someone to be healed?*

_____

_____

3. *When have you ever had to wait a long time to see an answer to prayer, and you were tempted to give up?*

_____

_____

4. *How can you look back and see God working in the situation?*

_____

_____

5. *Describe a time when God made a way for you to do or have something when, in the natural realm, it didn't look possible, yet you took a step of faith.*

_____

_____

6. *Do you struggle with thinking you have to be good enough or do more for God to do something for you?*

_____

_____

7. *Do you think you need more faith?*

_____

_____

8. *How does grace factor into that way of thinking?*

_____

_____

Final thought:

Jesus has all the faith we need and will give it to us when we need it.

Journal:

_____

_____

_____

_____

_____

_____

_____

_____

_____

_____

_____

_____

_____

_____

_____

_____

_____

_____

_____

_____

_____

_____

_____

_____

_____

_____

_____

_____

_____

_____

_____

_____

_____

_____

Lesson 11: Faith in Waiting

The Tabernacle in the wilderness is a picture of our life as believers.

The large curtain surrounding the courtyard of the Tabernacle has only one gate of entry, which represents Jesus as the Way. We can stop in the courtyard, but if we don't go any further, we only experience the Brazen Altar, which represents the Cross, in the Outer Court. This open area is lit by natural light and is a picture of the natural man. It represents our outer man, our body, or fleshly attitudes. Some people become born again (enter the gate) but never grow past their salvation experience. They seem content just to know Jesus as *Savior* but have no desire to know Him as *Lord*. This yields only about a 30% return on what Jesus has done for us. There is so much more beyond the Outer Court!

We can go further and take the next step. The priests had to wash in the Laver, which represents the Word. It was made from brass mirrors, enabling them to see their reflection in the water. The priests had to do this before they could go through the next doorway into the Holy Place.

This ceremonial washing is a picture of us when seeing our hearts reflected back to us as we allow the Word of God to reflect who we really are. This process both reveals and cleanses the sin in our hearts.

Next, the priests went through another doorway, crossing the threshold into the Holy Place where the Candlestick, the Bread of the Presence, and the Altar of Incense were. This represents where we begin to fellowship with other believers through prayer, represented by the Altar of Incense, and allowing the Holy Spirit to reveal the scripture to us, represented by the Candlestick. This symbolizes that His Word is a lamp unto our feet, a light to our path. We eat the bread together, represented by the Table of Showbread, as we fellowship around the Word. This also represents Communion because the wine was poured out here. This room represents where God deals with the soul. There is no natural light here; it was lit by the Candlestick or Menorah. Stopping here yields about a 60% return on what Jesus has done for us.

The Holy Place is when we interact with other believers while praying, allowing the Holy Spirit to reveal the scripture. By this, we renew our minds while we study the scriptures. As iron sharpens iron, God uses others to help us grow (Proverbs 27:17).

Finally, there is the Most Holy Place, behind the veil, where the presence of God is the only light, and you and God get down to business. He speaks to you one-on-one in a place of intimacy with Him, heart to heart. The Most Holy Place is where God deals with the spirit of man. This is where we practice the presence of God. The Ark of the Covenant now resides in our hearts. Entering this place yields a full 100% return on what God has invested in us. However, probably only a small percentage of Christians experience this (Mark 4:3-8).

Discussion:

When in your Christian journey have you experienced each of the three areas in the Tabernacle (Outer Court, Holy Place, Most Holy Place) resulting in spiritual growth?

As was mentioned in a previous lesson, when Jesus died, the veil separating man from the Most Holy Place was torn in two from top to bottom, giving us direct access to God. We no longer have to wait for a priest to go in once a year to make atonement and intercede for us because Jesus is our High Priest who is always making intercession for us. We have become a royal priesthood. We can go into the presence of God at any time.

(♡) **Jesus made it possible to live in His presence through His shed blood, reconciling us to God.**

Discussion:

When have you found yourself yearning for God's power but not His presence?

Prayer: *Lord, I repent of wanting your power more than I want your presence. Please teach me how to sit with You and enjoy your presence. Show me your heart for me and help me know how much You love me. Give me a desire for more of You in my life. Give me a revelation of grace and all that You did for me on the cross. Help me to give You one hundred percent return on your investment. Show me what that would look like. I pray my thoughts would be your thoughts and your ways my ways. Amen.*

Seeing the symbolism inherent in God's design of the Tabernacle, (on the following page), we can see illustrated three basic levels of Jesus' ministry. The Outer Court is a picture of Jesus ministering to the multitudes. He spoke to them in parables, and some understood and followed Him. The Holy Place symbolizes the twelve to whom He revealed mysteries more plainly. The Most High Place is where the three who had an intimate relationship with Him experienced the Mount of Transfiguration, representing the glory of God revealed in us.

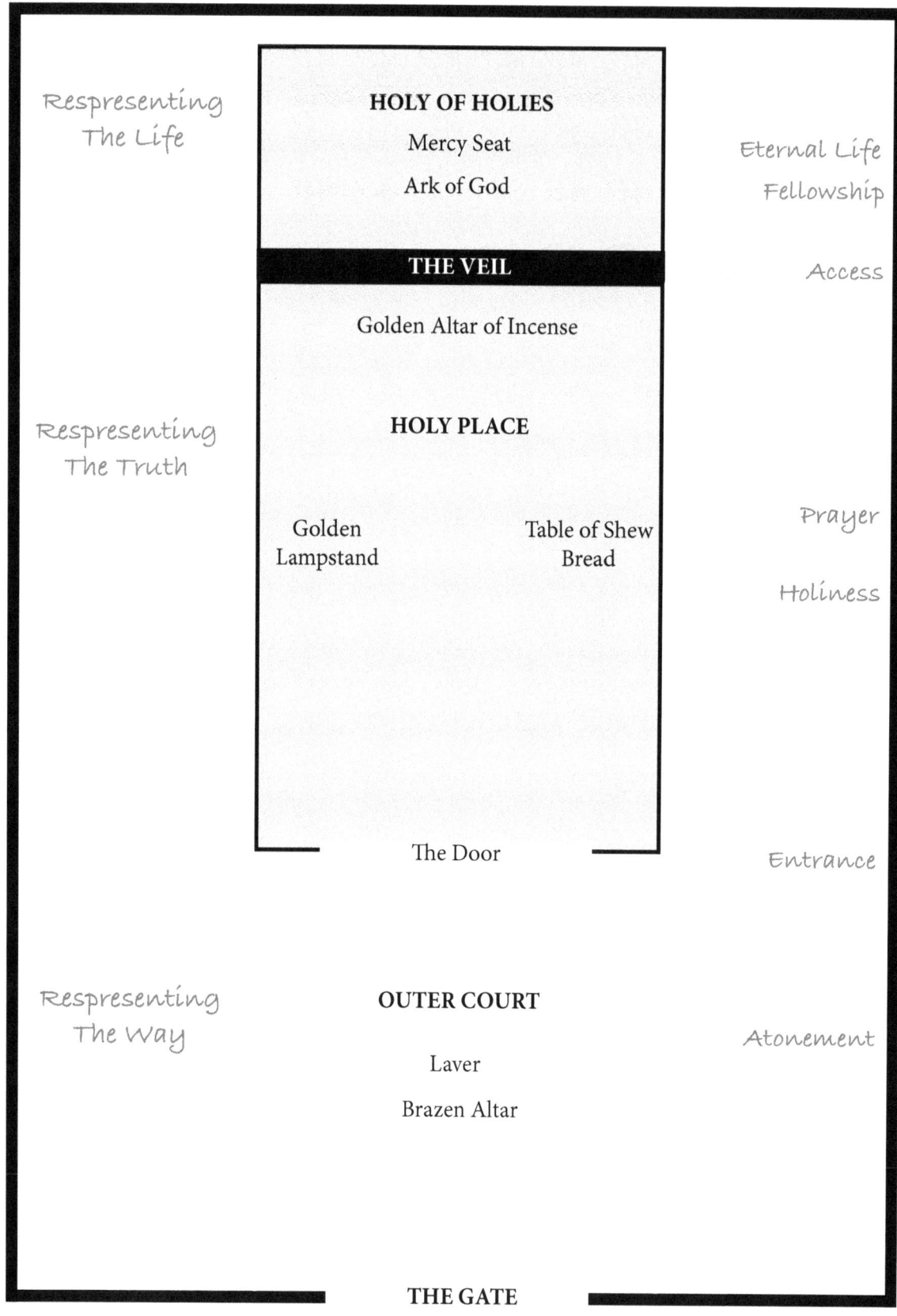

Respresenting
The Life

Eternal Life

Fellowship

Access

HOLY OF HOLIES

Mercy Seat

Ark of God

THE VEIL

Golden Altar of Incense

HOLY PLACE

Respresenting
The Truth

Prayer

Golden
Lampstand

Table of Shew
Bread

Holiness

The Door

Entrance

Respresenting
The Way

OUTER COURT

Atonement

Laver

Brazen Altar

THE GATE

⬭ **Planting: A seed of faith is like a mustard seed.**

The three areas of the Tabernacle could also represent man's spirit, soul, and body. When God gave instructions for the Tabernacle to be built, He began with the Ark of the Covenant, which represents the Spirit of God communing with the spirit of man. This is the ultimate destiny, but to be able to commune with God, man begins in the outer court at the Altar of salvation, the work of the cross.

A mustard seed looks like a tiny speck of ground pepper and can grow into a bush or tree (Mark 4:30-32). This growth takes time and patience, which are necessary elements to grow our faith as well. Hebrews 6:12: *through faith and patience we inherit the promises.* Patience shows true faith. Time is an unfailing test of faith. Time will remove what is not true and strengthen what is true.

⬭ **When our faith is in God, it will grow stronger regardless of the circumstances.**

If we don't wait on God's perfect timing, we will be tempted to take matters into our own hands. Abraham did this and ended up having Ishmael before Isaac. King Saul was also guilty of going his own way and lost his kingdom to David because of it. Ishmael was not who God promised Abraham and Sarah in Genesis 16. Saul was not God's best or in God's plan for Israel. The timing was off for a king (1 Samuel). The results in these stories illustrate living in the natural vs. the supernatural.

God has a plan and a purpose for each of our lives, but it requires waiting on His timing and not taking matters into our own hands. We can try to make it happen and receive a counterfeit, or we can wait on God to bring it about in His perfect timing. When we have a promise from God, we can trust Him to bring it to pass.

Sometimes we get impatient and try to "help" God. In doing this, we end up making a mess of things. The end result is what we bring about by natural means and self-effort. It is not the supernatural means where God gets all the glory, which is better by far.

Discussion:

How have you been guilty of doing this?

Our faith is like that mustard seed; God supplies it, and the life in the seed makes it grow. In the natural, it appears too small to become anything significant. We cannot will it to grow. But for it to be released from the grain, the outer shell has to break. That outer shell is the outer man that we call our soul, flesh, or natural man. So, for our spirit man to grow, we have to allow the Word of God to take root in our hearts.

Jesus is the Word made flesh. So, we receive His life and nature when we are born again. We are making an exchange, His life for ours. What does that look like? The Spirit of God is released through His Word. He brings the manifestation of what we believe. That is because the Word is alive and powerful as it lives in us. If we are not taught what the Bible says about our new spiritual life, how would we really know? We must invest in reading the scriptures.

Watering: *The seed is the Word of God.*

(Luke 8:11; Matthew 13:19) The Word of God contains the germ of eternal life. Romans 10:17: *faith comes by hearing, hearing by the word of Christ.* Find scriptures that apply to your situation and pray them out loud so they will go back down into your spirit and take root.

In Ephesians 5:26, it says *the Word washes us and transforms us*. He washes us, but we choose what we will wear. It's like on a cruise ship when you are invited to have dinner with the captain; you get dressed up. You wouldn't come into the dining room that night in just anything. With Christ, we put on robes of righteousness, humility, etc. (Job 29:14; Ephesians 6:14; Colossians 3:12). We get to wear the clothing and the perfume of a Bride (Psalms 45: 8,13-14). He provides it all, but whether or not we accept what He has provided is up to us.

Titus 3:5: *we are washed by regeneration and renewed by the Holy Spirit*. In Luke 8:11, it says that the seed sown is the Word of God. As a result, you will think differently. How do we water it? We water by meditating on the Word and remembering God's faithfulness (Galatians 3:3-5; Psalms 77:11-14). Our faith increases through obedience.

Fertilizer: This is the smelly part!

We don't always like what God uses to cause our faith to grow (James 1:1-12). Trials challenge our faith and are designed to produce spiritual maturity. It's just like when the stress of winter storms and summer droughts push a plant's roots deeper into the earth to find moisture, so too, our stressful times cause growth. When we know God will use trials for good, we will count it all as joy. We have to believe God is sovereign over everything — even trials.

Matthew 4:1-13 describes when Satan tested Jesus in the wilderness. The Holy Spirit led him into the wilderness, but it was not God; it was Satan who came to tempt Him. God allowed it, but Satan delivered the temptation. Satan also challenged His identity. He wants us to doubt what it means for us to be sons of God. Likewise, for us, Satan wants us to blame God for all our troubles.

In James 1:3, where it says *the testing of your faith produces patience*, the Greek word denotes a positive test intended to make one's faith "genuine." The result is steadfastness. We learn to live a life of faithful endurance amid troubles and afflictions. This kind of testing causes us to grow in holiness.

1 Peter 1:7: *so the genuineness of your faith is more valuable than gold, which perishes though refined by fire, may be found to result in praise and glory and honor at the revelation of Jesus Christ*

The crown of life literally referred to a laurel wreath worn by athletes and victorious emperors. In Revelation 2:10, we see that the reward of faithful endurance during tribulation is eternal life. Some of us might limp across the finish line, but what matters is that we finish the race.

Testing can become temptation instead of causing our character to be strengthened.

In James 1:14, the literal meaning of the word temptation is "lured and enticed." It is a fishing metaphor to draw a prey away from shelter to trap them with a deadly hook. Evil desire ensnares. God does not tempt us with evil.

Be careful you're not allowing your desires to be put before God's will because sometimes when we pray, we are praying for our will instead of God's (1 Peter 5:8-9).

Protect your faith by remembering it is because Jesus died for us that we experience grace. Watch for the enemy who will come to steal, kill, and destroy the growth and revelation the

Holy Spirit is bringing to you. The enemy will come in the form of fear, doubt, and unbelief. We have to weed these out of the soil because they will quench the Spirit (John 10:10).

The sin of unforgiveness is a weed that will keep your circumstances from changing. If we know the love of God, we know that He gave His Son for us so we could receive forgiveness. Therefore, how can we not forgive others? If He forgave us when we were the ones who blew it, the least we can do is forgive others. In fact, it is dangerous not to forgive others (Matthew 18:21-25).

Offenses stem from unforgiveness and will damage our faith. It is bait Satan uses to trap us in a spiritually vulnerable place. Everything we see and do will be filtered through a lens of offense. Harboring an offense causes us to focus on the negative instead of the positive (Proverbs 19:11; Matthew 15:21-28).

Prayer: *Father, show me if I am harboring an offense against anyone. Help me to repent and forgive anyone I feel has offended me. Lord, I ask you to bless them and show me how to do "good" to them and help me to love them* (Matthew 5:44-48).

The best way to protect your heart is through praise and worship, which brings in the presence of God. It takes time for the seed to come up where it can be seen, so worshiping and praising God in the midst of your circumstances will bring joy while you wait. In Galatians 5:22, it tells us that self-control (making right choices) is a fruit, or by-product, of the Holy Spirit. Therefore, when we choose to worship in the midst of our circumstances, we allow the Holy Spirit to be in control.

God Moment

Ask God to help you move into all He has for you.

Do you ever wonder if there is more? Do you long for it? Are you frustrated and worn out with struggling? Have you felt My gentle push nudging you forward?

You see that field with tape around it cautioning you to keep out. I'm encouraging you to move forward past the caution signs. They say, "Don't enter here." You want to, but you are afraid because you think you'll get in trouble and not be qualified to break through and stand where I'm calling you. But you long to see what is there. Go on in; I've given you the title deed. It's yours to possess.

The tape is an illusion of lies the enemy has wrapped around your mind to keep you from possessing the land. He knows your potential if you ever enter the Land of Promise. That place is prepared especially for you. Stop striving in the wrong field. There is treasure waiting here. It has your name on it. Take a moment. Trust Me; it's yours.

Isaiah 14:2

Numbers 34:2

Ezekiel 36:24

Ephesians 1:1

Assignment:

1. *Are you involved in more than just coming to church on Sunday (Outer Court)?*

_____

_____

2. *In order to grow spiritually, which area do you need to better engage?*

_____

_____

3. *So, what do you want your yield to be? Do you want thirty, sixty or a hundred-fold? What would that look like in your life?*

_____

_____

Journal:

_____

_____

_____

_____

_____

_____

_____

_____

_____

_____

_____

_____

_____

_____

_____

_____

_____

_____

_____

_____

_____

_____

_____

_____

_____

_____

_____

_____

_____

_____

_____

_____

_____

_____

_____

_____

_____

Lesson 12: Faith in Action

🜂 **Pruning:** *It is with the heart men believe* (Romans 10:10).

The Word is alive and powerful. When we hear scripture, it brings life to us. It divides the soul and the spirit and discerns the intents of the heart (Hebrews 4:12).

Discussion:

Can you name something you've been convicted to cut out in your life to allow new growth in other areas? Has God ever had to do it for you?

In Genesis 3:22-24, the Cherubim are a picture of the Holy Spirit guarding the way into the garden and the presence of God until Jesus accomplishes the work of the cross. The faces on the Cherubim reflect the nature of Christ. He wants to transform us into His image. Now, through his death and resurrection, we have been given a way into the presence of God. In John 20:12, we see the two witnesses in the two Angels who are at the head and feet of Jesus. This reminds us of the two cherubim guarding the entrance to the Garden and also on the Mercy Seat watching over the Word.

Jesus has performed the Word, so now we have a way to discern truth. As we allow the Word of God to divide between the soul and the spirit, we will be changed into the image of Christ. The flaming sword is the word of God that is given to build character.

Hebrews 4:12: *for the Word of God is living and effective and sharper than any double-edged sword, penetrating as far as the separation of soul and spirit, joints, and marrow. It is able to judge between the thoughts and intents of the heart. (HCSB)*

Dross is waste matter. It contains the impurities that are burned away in the process of refining or smelting metals, especially gold.

Similarly, we are purified, refined, and transformed as the Word of God, if it is allowed to have its perfect work, burns away the dross.

Another example of being refined and transformed is creating pottery and the process called "Raku," which requires multiple firings. These firings remind us of the fire of God perfecting us through trials. Each firing results in more brilliant color and beauty.

However, Satan's goal continues to be to separate us from the love of God. We have to guard our hearts so the enemy cannot plant seeds of distrust toward the Lord. It will not only separate us from the presence of God but will also separate us from the Body of Christ. When the enemy tries to sow seeds of doubt, we have to agree with what the Word of God says about the situation and about who we are in Christ.

Your soul has to cooperate, and your flesh has to be broken for what is inside to come forth. It will cost our flesh something to worship at the feet of Jesus. Our flesh, like the alabaster box, has to be broken to have intimacy with Jesus (Mark 14:3). This is easier said than done. Each discipline of the Holy Spirit is to break our outward man (flesh) so our inward man (spirit) can come through empowered by the Holy Spirit. This is when, like the alabaster box, we release a pleasing aroma to the Lord (2 Corinthians 2:15). Our relationship with Him must be more precious to us than what our flesh wants to do.

Perception:

Sometimes pruning comes through trials and tribulations (Acts 14:22). If we want to be all God wants us to be, there are things we have to allow Him to weed out of our lives when we are unwilling or hesitant to let go and take care of it ourselves. Maybe the dross is hidden so deep in our souls that we don't even know it is there. God will bring specific circumstances which cause the dross to surface and make us aware of our need for healing. Once we know the need is there, we have to deal with it to continue on the spiritual journey God has for us. Pruning removes whatever inhibits spiritual growth in our lives and enables us to bear fruit. Repentance is the goal of pruning.

The goal of God's discipline is also to bring us to repentance. God disciplines us to correct, chastise, or prevent us from harmful sin. He weeds out pride, idolatry, and presumptions. We must be sure we don't become bitter because things didn't turn out the way we wanted (Hebrews 12:5-13).

Romans 8:28 says God promises *that all things will work together for good for those who are called according to His purpose.* Therefore, we can always trust God because He is good.

Let faith be a shield.

Faith believes God is good all the time, even when circumstances don't line up with what we believe. When faced with challenging circumstances, first look at what God says about it. Remember the Christian teaching that *facts lead, faith follows,* and *feelings bring up the rear.* When it gets personal, we tend to let our feelings rule instead of shielding our hearts with faith in God's promises (Mark 4:26-29).

This scripture encourages us not to dig up the seed to see if it is growing. Instead, though we have no physical evidence anything is happening, we wait for God to bring new life.

Faith increases when we are living under His authority.

Understanding authority is important to living a life of faith. An example is in Matthew 8:5-10 when the Centurion asked Jesus to speak the Word so his servant would be healed. He understood Jesus' authority in the spirit realm. Exercising authority requires a servant's heart. Biblical authority goes vertical first, from our hearts to God's, then horizontal to those around you in your sphere of influence. Faith comes when we are living life under His authority and not under our own. Jesus said to the Centurion: *I have not seen faith as great as this.*

Faith is the substance (title deed/realization) of things hoped for, the evidence (confidence/conviction) of things not seen Hebrews 11:1.

Faith consists of persistent hope in the promises of God, especially when we don't see them at the moment.

Belief is a mental realm of thought; faith is action.

🫶 **It is not about how much faith we have. It's about letting Him impart His faith to us.**

Faith is a gift to me.

Faith always has in it the idea of action—movement towards its object. It is the soul leaping forth to embrace and take a promise or belief as yours, whether you see it yet or not. We

144

can have belief without faith. Faith puts belief into active service and connects possibilities with actualities. Faith is acting on what you believe. You appropriate it when you take something for your own use. If you believe it, you will speak it (2 Corinthians 4:13-14).

An example given is when you observe a chair. You believe the chair will hold you if you sit down in it. You demonstrate the belief when you actually sit down and trust it to hold your weight.

In John 21:15-17 the words for love are *phileo* (friend) and *agape* (divine) love. Peter began with a fond affection for the Lord; however, Jesus still called him into ministry. He knew Peter hadn't reached a place of loving Him or others out of agape love. That kind of love comes from faith working out of love. It is a gift of grace that Jesus will impart to us when we answer the call. It doesn't originate in the natural realm but in the supernatural realm. Only the Holy Spirit living in us can bring about that kind of love in our hearts.

Discussion:

What causes you to feel that you don't have enough faith?

The Power Gifts are listed in 1 Corinthians 12.

Gift of Faith: This is the power to believe and accompanies most of the gifts (Matthew 14:28-33). Faith believes with your heart and not just your head. The heart is the whole man (*i.e.,* intellect, will, and senses).

The gift of faith is special faith, supernaturally given at a time of need. It can happen when the Holy Spirit gives you an understanding of the will of God in a situation.

The gift of faith is a supernatural confidence that God is going to move in a situation to bring change (job, health, family). We find examples of this in Daniel 3 when Daniel, was placed in the lion's den. We see it again in 1 Kings 18:2-45 when Elijah said it would rain.

Jesus prayed for Lazarus (John 11:39-44) to be raised from the dead and had the supernatural ability to combat doubt and unbelief with an inner conviction. The gift of faith defies logic and natural reality for a higher spiritual reality.

It causes natural things to line up with what God has already accomplished supernaturally.

Miracles: By definition, a miracle is something that happens beyond natural means. A friend of mine, the late John Dee, had a video of a man being raised from the dead back to life in Africa. He had already been embalmed. *That* is a miracle!

Miracles come from a power beyond human means, interrupting natural laws, like addiction with no withdrawal when set free, for example. Miracles bring authority over sin, Satan, and sickness by bringing healing and deliverance.

Miracles are supernatural acts of God by the Spirit. They fall under the category of signs and wonders and are designed to increase faith. Just to name a few: the conception of Jesus in Luke 1:37, the Exodus and the Red Sea parting, Elisha prophesied the woman's child and later raised him from the dead (2 Kings 4:16-37), Paul healed and delivered people in Acts 19:11-12, Jesus' first miracle was turning water into wine (John 2:1-11).

Gifts of Healings: Faith is usually the prerequisite for healings to manifest (Matthew 8).

Healings may happen without human aid or by medical means with divine assistance.

 **Results have nothing to do with us.**

There are three kinds of healings: Instant, progressive, and obedient. Examples include the healing of a blind man in Mark 10:51-52, the healing of another blind man in Mark 8:22-25, and obedient healings like in 2 Kings 5:10-12.

The blind man healed in John 9:6-7 is an example of the natural and supernatural working together.

Naaman, the leper, was healed but required to do something (2 Kings 5:10-12).

The Bible also tells us two other ways:

1. Call for the elders to pray in faith (James 5:14).

2. Confess your sins to one another that you may be healed (James 5:16).

God Moment:

Ask God for the faith to believe that He is answering your prayers.

My yoke is easy, and My burden is light. If you are laboring under a spirit of heaviness, confusion, and despair, I did not ask you to carry what is on your back. You are carrying someone else's burden, and it's too heavy for you. You will not be able to stand under the load.

You have allowed other people to put their problems on you. You were never meant to carry their burden. Give it to Me, and I will take care of it. Don't be anxious.

Take a moment and begin to release it by praising me. Trust me to take care of it. I want you to be free.

Isaiah 58:6

Matthew 11:30

Galatians 5:1

Assignment:

1. When has it been the hardest for you to believe God?

_____

_____

2. Describe a time when you felt God gave you supernatural faith concerning something?

_____

_____

Final thought:

Living a life of faith is living supernaturally naturally. Faith brings spiritual growth in the Christian life. Faith is a gift!

Journal:

_____

_____

_____

_____

_____

_____

_____

_____

_____

_____

_____

_____

_____

_____

_____

_____

_____

_____

_____

_____

_____

_____

_____

_____

_____

_____

_____

_____

_____

_____

_____

_____

_____

_____

Journal:

_____

_____

_____

_____

_____

_____

_____

_____

_____

_____

_____

_____

_____

_____

_____

_____

_____

_____

_____

_____

_____

_____

_____

_____

_____

_____

_____

_____

_____

_____

_____

Appendix:

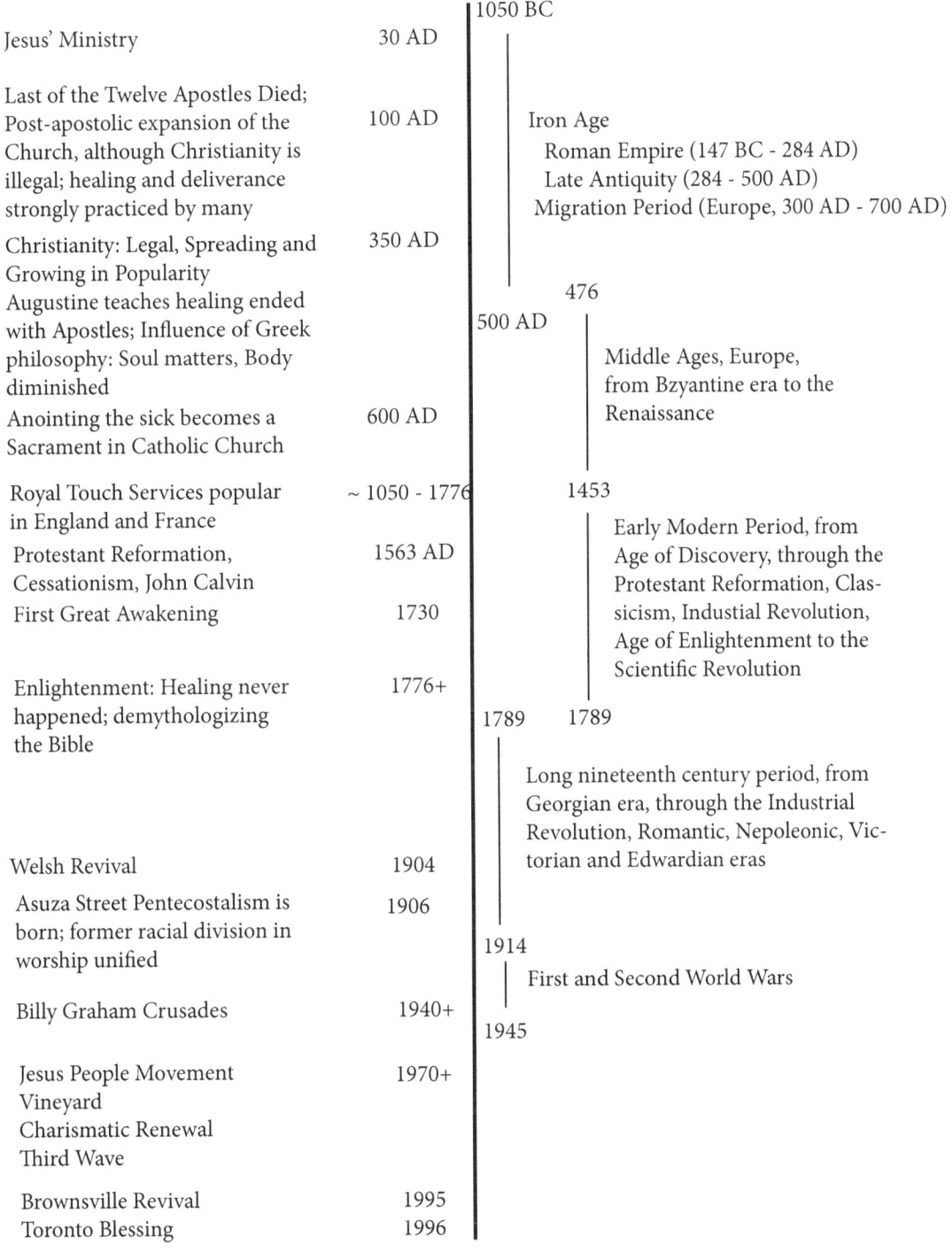

The Church

The World

1050 BC

Jesus' Ministry — 30 AD

Last of the Twelve Apostles Died; Post-apostolic expansion of the Church, although Christianity is illegal; healing and deliverance strongly practiced by many — 100 AD

Iron Age
  Roman Empire (147 BC - 284 AD)
  Late Antiquity (284 - 500 AD)
  Migration Period (Europe, 300 AD - 700 AD)

Christianity: Legal, Spreading and Growing in Popularity — 350 AD

Augustine teaches healing ended with Apostles; Influence of Greek philosophy: Soul matters, Body diminished

476

500 AD

Anointing the sick becomes a Sacrament in Catholic Church — 600 AD

Middle Ages, Europe, from Bzyantine era to the Renaissance

Royal Touch Services popular in England and France — ~ 1050 - 1776

1453

Protestant Reformation, Cessationism, John Calvin — 1563 AD

First Great Awakening — 1730

Early Modern Period, from Age of Discovery, through the Protestant Reformation, Classicism, Industial Revolution, Age of Enlightenment to the Scientific Revolution

Enlightenment: Healing never happened; demythologizing the Bible — 1776+

1789   1789

Long nineteenth century period, from Georgian era, through the Industrial Revolution, Romantic, Nepoleonic, Victorian and Edwardian eras

Welsh Revival — 1904

Asuza Street Pentecostalism is born; former racial division in worship unified — 1906

1914

First and Second World Wars

Billy Graham Crusades — 1940+

1945

Jesus People Movement
Vineyard
Charismatic Renewal
Third Wave — 1970+

Brownsville Revival — 1995
Toronto Blessing — 1996

How Did the Mainstream Church "Lose" the Gifts of the Spirit?
A short history of deliverance and healing

2 Timothy 3:5: *Having the appearance of godliness, but denying its power …*

v. 16–17: *…All Scripture is breathed out by God and profitable for teaching, reproof, for correction and for training.*

God ordained the Ten Commandments and 613 other instructions and procedures that together are called Mosaic Law, which came through Moses to the people. But by the time Jesus was born, literally thousands of additional laws had been added to "clarify" what God meant by what He originally said.

Jesus was not impressed. In Matthew 23:27-28, He said: *"Woe to you, teachers of the law and Pharisees, you hypocrites! You are like whitewashed tombs, which look beautiful on the outside but on the inside are full of the bones of the dead and everything unclean. In the same way, on the outside you appear to people as righteous, but on the inside, you are full of hypocrisy and wickedness.*

So today, even with the Holy Spirit, it isn't a big surprise that today's Christians, too, are subject to errors of addition or omission as we practice our faith. These alterations have evolved over time, generations, and cultures, as well-meaning leaders have added to or taken away from what Jesus taught. As the old hymn lyric laments, *"Prone to wander, Lord I feel it, Prone to leave the God I love…"*

Using this understanding of our human proclivity as a background, let's look back at how the Spiritual Gifts of tongues, healing, and deliverance, once so central to Christian life during the first century (as described in Acts), came to be so sidelined, scorned, or ignored by the twenty-first century.

Historical Refresher

Historically, Jesus lived, and the Church evolved, first during the Iron Age, roughly 1050 BC – 500 AD. This was followed by the Middle, or "Dark" Ages, 476 – 1453 AD, which ended with the Renaissance, which started about 1300.

Just as today's Church is influenced by the culture of the day (think about traditional vs contemporary music styles, "seeker" services, "felt needs" programming, and an almost complete banning of political discourse from the pulpit due to tax laws regarding churches' non-profit status, etc.) so too, were churches, church leaders, and trends influenced by the context of their cultures — despite Jesus' warning about the "leaven of the Pharisees" (Matthew 16:12). As we look at the larger environment, make up your own mind as to whether certain elements of change were founded in the prevailing culture, or by divine revelation.

The Middle Ages were followed by the early modern period, which began with the Age of Discovery (aka the Age of Exploration) around 1400, continued through the Protestant Reformation in the 16th century, the first Industrial Revolution in Europe, the Age of Enlightenment (or Reason), and the Scientific Revolution in the 18th century. That just hits the highlights of history, but its enough to give you a background.

Now let's "zoom in" to map the changes in the practice of Christianity during those time periods.

By the fourth century, the beginning of the Early Middle Ages, it had become unfashionable to practice healing, or even pray for the sick, the reasoning being that to do so was prideful. Those who did so were judged to think so highly of themselves as to be worthy of sainthood. Of course, this thinking reflects a false humility that directly contradicts Paul's teaching in 1 Corinthians 12:4-30.

Given the lack of medical treatments and the acute awareness of evil spirits, monsters, and other non-human creatures in the world, it is incredible that Christianity in particular, voluntarily gave up practicing the delegated power Jesus Himself had assigned to His followers so they would be able to overcome the havoc rendered by such evil.

As Christianity spread and became more the norm throughout the Western world, it also carried with it less of the disrupting, influential power it once commonly displayed when it was practiced by an outlier group of radicals in the first century.

Too Emotional?

The enduring criticism by "mainstream Christians" and others of those groups still (or again) practicing the Gifts of the Spirit is that they are "too emotional," an assertion that still dogs the Church today. It's just not sophisticated to submit fully, including your heart and emotions, to a wild, living, and unpredictable God. This, too, has roots in the Old Testament. (See 2 Samuel 6:14-16). Emotions, like human relationships involving them, can be messy. But returning to Scripture, isn't this what God wants? A passionate, heart-to-Heart relationship with us, including our hearts (emotions), bodies, minds, and strength?

By the eighth century, the latter part of the Early Middle Ages, baptism was mostly performed on babies, rarely on adults, and expectations of what it meant to live a life of faith further diminished.

From Common Practice to Exclusively the Elite

According to author Francis MacNutt, in his book, *The Nearly Perfect Crime,* "Gradually, [manifestations of the Holy Spirit] became the exception; visions and healings came to be associated with especially holy people. Instead of the charismatic gifts being seen as ordinary, they came to be seen as rare and as proof that a Christian was deserving of sainthood. ... If you disconnect any belief in the source of it all, the power of the Spirit, you naturally disconnect any belief in its effects, such as healing the sick. By the year 800 — more or less — a desire for baptism with the Holy Spirit had disappeared, although individuals throughout the ages still experienced its reality. ...But when Christianity saw itself as triumphant, the need for miracles as proof died out."

Resurgence through Royalty

However, from the eleventh to early nineteenth centuries, the "Royal Touch" was established and practiced in both France and England. (Looking back at our timeline, this started in the Middle Ages, and continued into the Early Modern Period.) These popular healing services were based on the belief that the monarchs, having been anointed by God, had the power to heal the commoners with their touch. Thousands would flock to the events, and as often happens when power and politics meet, there was a large amount of corruption involved as the services were abused. Calvin observed these abuses and was consequently influenced against the practice of the Royal Touch Services, as well as the practices of healing and deliverance in general. The monarchs' motivations were often rooted more in proving their divine authority than in actually caring about those they ruled. MacNutt credits the influence of Calvinism for ending the royal healing services in 1688 in England, and in 1825 (during the French Revolution) in France.

Keep in mind, these services were stopped as the Industrial Revolution and Age of Enlightenment (or Age of Reason) were taking place. Even though the Scientific Revolution was still a century or so to come, many Christians started to "intellectualize" their belief in the basic tenants of the faith, coming to see the Bible as myth and legend rather than historically true. The Christian faith had been sanitized into something the masses could understand and accept, but largely lost its power.

Picking Up What Augustine Put Down: Cessation

In his early days, St. Augustine and, on a more lukewarm level, Roman Catholic Church espoused the idea of Cessationism, the idea that the Gifts of the Spirit ended with the death of the last Apostle. The Catholic Church still believed in miracles, but that they were rare. St. Augustine later retracted his belief in the idea in his book, *Retractions*, and admitted he had been wrong. Calvin, however, ignored Augustine's rejection of cessationism and doubled down on it, crystalizing it into a formal doctrine. MacNutt commented: "For Calvin, miracles were not just rare: They ended with the death of the last apostle. He believed in every miracle described in the New Testament, but after that, it was over. … How ironic that healing and deliverance, so central to Jesus' preaching, were totally done away with by the Protestant Reformation … the very ones who were most devoted to the Word of God and championed its literal interpretation came to believe that God meant healing to last only for those early apostolic days."

By the eighteenth century, scientific findings had been positioned as opposing faith beliefs as man elevated his own intellect above God's word, and eventually, groups considering themselves to be liberal Christians came to view the biblical accounts of miracles as myth rather than truth. This is when the divide began to emerge between the two groups of Protestant Christians, the "conservatives" who believed the miracles as recounted in the Bible actually happened but no longer occurred, and the "liberals" who believed they were purely fiction.

As you can imagine, the latter viewpoint appeals more to the highly educated, intellectual crowd who view healings and other gifts of the Spirit as relics of an uneducated populace. Dispensationalists contributed to this view, the idea that historically, there are several eras wherein the charisma, or gifts of the Spirit, were present, (such as in biblical times); but that we now live in a different dispensation, where they are essentially dead.

Mainstream Christian thought leaders such as Rudolf Bultmann (1888-1976) continued and built on the belief that biblical accounts of healings and miracles were impossible, even delusional, and that the biggest miracle on which Christianity is built, the Resurrection, did not happen in a literal sense.

Revivals of Spiritual Gifts Opposed from Within

Jonathan Edwards, well-known Puritan preacher, in 1734 was a conduit along with his powerful sermons of a famous revival in Northampton, Massachusetts. Gifts of the spirit were manifested, and as too often happens, he was soundly criticized for it from those within his own denomination. The overwhelming presence of God's glory, and parishioners being "slain in the spirit" was considered not a sign of God's hand in the meetings, but of an over-emotional and unbalanced ministry. In response to his many critics, Edwards admitted that the Northampton revival showed some excesses. Afterwards, the revival activity in his congregation greatly diminished, although he continued to receive wide recognition for his writings. Incidentally, one of the criticisms leveled at his ministry was the audacity that laypeople, rather than exclusively clergy, could minister to and pray for each other. It was a radical idea at the time, and causes one to wonder how else have we as Christians thwarted or grieved the Spirit? Fortunately, we serve a God who looks at the heart.

There were many other instances of revival across the world. (See timeline).

Most who seek to change culture in any form, face initial opposition, and such has been true throughout the Western world as it concerns Christianity. Again, I would ask you to do your own prayer and research in sorting out the Spiritual Gifts and their place in your faith and life in Christ. Start with:

Matthew 10:1(NIV): Jesus called his twelve disciples to him and gave them authority to drive out impure spirits and to heal every disease and sickness. (Also detailed in Luke 9:1)

Matthew 10:7-8: As you go, proclaim this message: 'The kingdom of heaven has come near. Heal the sick, raise the dead, cleanse those who have leprosy, drive out demons. Freely you have received; freely give.'

I'll end with another of MacNutt's observations that:

"… Jesus shared with us His own divine power to heal the sick. First He gave it to the Twelve, then to the 72, and finally, since Pentecost, to everyone who chooses to believe and follow Him. The major teaching summing up the entire book of Acts is that God equipped those early followers to do the very same things Jesus did. First they proclaimed to everyone that the Kingdom of God was present, truly in our midst. Then they demonstrated the Kingdom of God by healing the sick and freeing those held captive by evil spirits.

"Without the twin ministries of healing and deliverance, our preaching that God's Kingdom is here and that Satan's dominion is being destroyed is hollow."

Scriptures regarding Spiritual Gifts:

1 Corinthians 14:31-32: The spirit of the prophet is subject to the prophet. We can control our tongue. We have a choice about whether or not we speak. The Cliché: "know about all you tell but don't tell all you know. Sometimes we are not to pass on all God has revealed to us, we are just supposed to pray about it.

1 Corinthians 14:39-40: Desire earnestly to prophesy, but do not forbid speaking with tongues. Just do it in a way to assure order.

Recommended Reading for Further Study

Bevere, John. *The Bait of Satan*. Lake Mary: Charisma House, 2004.

Bridges, Jerry. *The Discipline of Grace: God's Role and Our Role in the Pursuit of Holiness*. Carol Stream: NavPress, 1994.

Evans, William. *The Great Doctrines of the Bible*. Melbourne: Book Jungle, 2009.

Grubb, Norman. *The Key to Everything*. Fort Washington: CLC Ministries, 1985.

Hayford, Jack. *The Beauty of Spiritual Language*. Nashville: Thomas Nelson, 1996.

MacNutt, Francis. *The Nearly Perfect Crime*. Grand Rapids: Chosen Books, 2005.

Morris, Henry. Dr. *The Genesis Record*. Grand Rapids: Baker Book House, 1976.

Nee, Watchman. *The Spiritual Man*. Fort Washington: CLC Ministries, 1968.

Whyte, Maxwell. *The Power of the Blood*. New Kensington: Whittaker House, 1973.